Dear
Barbara,
May God's wor[d]
blessings con[t]
to flow to
completio[n]
thank you
In Christ
Joy

Patricia Joy

DELIVERANCE
The Christian's Bill Of Rights

DELIVERANCE
The Christian's Bill Of Rights

Patricia Joy

WINEPRESS WP PUBLISHING

This book is dedicated to
Pastor Paul Carroll,
who laid down his life
for the Church
and this teaching.

He now resides
in the heavenlies
with the Lord Jesus Christ.

Contents

FOREWORD

I lie awake in the darkness distraught and depressed. An unholy dread consumes me and leaves me without hope. A thought comes to mind: *End your worthless life.* The oppression is so heavy upon me that I continue to lie motionless. I cry out to God, "Help me, please!" Suddenly, an awakening thought triggers my body into motion as I sit up in bed, alert and listening. The thoughts flood my mind as a revelation. *Wait a minute, I would never take my life! That is against God. He created me. That is worth something. What right do I have to kill what He made!* I begin to look around with spiritual eyes. *Who's there?* I pondered. *Where is this evil influence coming from?* I asked myself.

In the following weeks I would strive to seek knowledge and truth. I knew it was wrong to be so miserable and was willing to do what was right to be set free. Shortly after I gave my life to God, through Jesus Christ, I was led by some dear friends into the dining room of the most remarkable couple, the pastors of the Church in San Diego, Paul and Patricia Carroll.

The love that emanated from them was so pure, I knew that it must be Jesus in them. This love created a comfortable atmosphere of trust. Their genuine concern for my well-being and their ability to ask questions that would draw out troubled areas of my life indicated that there was a higher authority working through them. Only the Holy Spirit could enable someone to see my heart. As we sat around their table, they walked me through a brief history of my youth and current family situation and were able to discern demonic influences that were a torment to me. After the discussion they held my hands and Paul earnestly prayed to the Father for all of my needs, as well as the needs of my friends and family members.

After prayer, Patricia laid hands on my head and began calling out the specific devils that were causing the difficulties in my life. It was an unusual experience as I felt a release and a cleansing take place. For the first time in my life I was able to truly do something to make a change for the better, and, best of all (and this always makes me cry), there were people who not only cared enough to help me, but truly knew how. This was a true miracle in my life.

That day I left their house a new person. I felt free from the entanglements of the evil influences that exist in the spiritual realm and, most importantly, I received knowledge that would help me to stay that way!

Before I went to them for this deliverance, Patricia encouraged me to listen to the audio cassettes of a series of studies on deliverance that she had taught to the Church in San Diego before I joined them. Listening to the studies helped me understand the strongholds that Satan and his cohorts are able to have on people. Listening to these studies prepared my heart to desire deliverance. It helped me discover that beneath the rough exterior of a troubled life was a sincere person seeking the truth and love of God. This helped me to not only love myself again, but to love others, for I began to see people in a new way. Instead of thinking, "That person is no good," I began thinking, "God created that person, but look what the evil, demonic influences have done." This gave me compassion for people and a willingness to pray for them and bring the knowledge to them that they don't have to be in bondage to unhappiness.

What a blessing that these studies are now available in book form, as the teachings can be better utilized to bring light to spiritual eyes, allowing us to fight our worst enemy with confidence and hope. I am very excited about this book, because I know it will serve as a priceless component to the Christian who is desiring a deeper, more meaningful walk with Jesus Christ. Not only will the reader benefit from the precious wisdom of these teachings, but also those around him.

Every time I would say thank you to Pastor Paul or Pastor Patricia they would react the same way. They would look up and say, "Don't thank me; thank Him." And I do, I do!! I never met anyone before who was so willing to give of himself or herself for others, and this gave me a desire to someday do for others what they did for me. I esteem God highly for the work done through Pastors Paul and Patricia Carroll, and I praise Him for the love that made it possible to "set the captives free"!

CHAPTER ONE

LAYING DOWN THE FOUNDATION

(THE POWER WE HAVE BEEN GIVEN)

To comprehend the things of God, one must have a depth of knowledge and understanding of the activity taking place in the spiritual realm. Through the ages, there have been those in the Church who have continued to believe that Christians can be "demon-possessed." However, there have been others, who, through the teachings of alleged modern schools of theology, have accepted materialistic ideas and concepts rather than spiritual. Thus they have substituted and confused the acts of demonization and possession with emotional and mental impairment, and therefore have been greatly deceived.

In the original Greek, the word *possessed* means, "to be exercised by a demon, to have or to be vexed[1] with, a devil [demon]." People have mistakenly understood the word possess to mean total ownership. Consequently, most of the

Church has denied the fact that Christians can have devils. The denial of demon spirits, or devils, has caused a great darkness to fall upon the Church. This deception continues because of a lack of knowledge of the word possess.

The question most often raised is, "How can you have the Holy Spirit and Jesus residing in you *and* have a devil or devils?" Regardless of professed modern theology, a Christian can have an indwelling devil as an undesirable trespasser. To stress the importance of this point, I repeat: A Christian *can* have an indwelling devil as an undesirable trespasser. It is of utmost importance that I stress this point to you, as you will be questioned sternly when you begin operating in this spiritual knowledge. This understanding is not as prevalent as it should be in the Church. You must have a ready answer when questioned—and you *will* be questioned.

A trespasser is one who unlawfully comes upon the territory of another. In the case of a Christian, it is unlawful for Satan or his devils to trespass. In the case of an unbeliever, it is lawful. Why is it unlawful for Satan and his devils to trespass upon a Christian? Because we, as Christians, have received redemption and were purchased by the precious and all-powerful blood of Christ.[2] Therefore, the Devil has no legal right to trespass upon the Christian. However, the Devil and his devils will continue to trespass and perform their unlawful practices until they are confronted and challenged legally on the basis of your legal rights as the redeemed through the blood of Christ. If you are ignorant of your legal rights, Satan and his devils will wreak havoc upon your life.

Look around you! Can we deny what we see before our very eyes all the time? Oh, beloved, look at the continually painful situations that plague us because devils have invaded our people: divorce, child abuse, sickness and disease, and constant frustration, hatred, and anger. Can we deny that these situations exist in the Church? Did not Satan come to steal, destroy, and kill?[3] Satan will stop at nothing to influence us toward evil, the consequence of which is destruction. If we allow him to get away with this, Satan will continue his unlawful practices upon the Church until he is confronted and challenged on the basis of our legal rights.

All Christians should know what their legal rights are. What I have witnessed in my experiences with most Christians is that, either by choice or by incorrect teaching, they do not know what their legal rights are in the spiritual kingdom. This is most regrettable. I am speaking of spiritual law here—spiritual rights—legalities a Christian must know if he is to be victorious over evil.

You know that as a Christian you have been bought; you have been purchased with the blood of Jesus Christ.[4] When Satan and his devils come, they are trespassing on territory that is already owned, and they have no legal right to move on property already purchased. We have been commissioned and given by God the power and right to protect this property and to drive out and keep Satan out. Unfortunately, we have been unaware of Satan's tactics of deception and of our rights and authority. The Bible tells us of our rights in Revelation 22:14: *"Blessed are they that do his commandments, that they may have right to the tree of life, and may enter in through the gates into the city"* (KJV). However, we have been told by the world and the Church that our problems can be coped with, and that, in fact, our hope is found in trusting our spiritual selves to psychologists and psychology. Psychologists deal only with the mind with great uncertainty and limited knowledge, when all along the problems they've been trying to solve are not mental but spiritual.

In Ephesians 6:12 the Bible tells us, *"For our struggle is not against flesh and blood, but against . . . the world forces of this darkness, against the spiritual forces of wickedness in the heavenly places"* (NASB). If the psychologists were aware of what they were dealing with in the spiritual realm, and they had the saving knowledge and authority of the Word, their work would be more profound and successful, not to mention much quicker. However, very few do have this knowledge which comes from the Holy Spirit, so there are throngs of people going to psychologists and psychiatrists for long periods of time at great cost and with little or no success. I am also referring to Christian counselors. One would think that Christian counseling would be more successful than secular counseling.

I want you to understand and know your legal rights, and to know that this redemption can be a quick work. To know that you can be totally set free and remain free is an extraordinary and exciting fact, one that the Church in general has not considered. So, you see, the Devil has no legal rights to the Christian, but it is up to the Christian to defend his rights for which Christ has already paid. The dilemma is that the Christian is not taking an active role in protecting his rights, mostly because of the poor, erroneous teaching that the responsibility is not his, but Christ's alone. This inaccurate teaching has caused a lack of spiritual knowledge. Hosea 4:6 states, *"My people are destroyed for a lack of knowledge . . . ."*

We see the bitter fruits all around us that stem from incorrect teaching.

Now, no devil can remain in a Christian if that Christian seriously desires the devil to go. James 4:7 states, *". . . Resist the devil and he will flee from you."* This can be done either by yourself, if you have the strength and knowledge of the Word, or through the help of a knowledgeable Christian brother.

The question often asked is, "Do we as Christians have the right to cast out devils, or did this power belong only to the original twelve apostles?" Many denominations believe this power was granted only to the apostles by Jesus. However, Mark 16:17 clearly states, *"And these signs shall follow them that believe; In My name shall they cast out devils . . ."* (KJV). Therefore, if you believe in the name of Jesus, you not only have the right, but you have the power. It must be understood that "them that believe" are those who have unquestionable faith in what Jesus Christ declared is true yesterday, today, and, yes, forever.[5]

Let's examine Mark 16:18. It says, *"They shall take up serpents; and . . . it shall not hurt them . . . ."* Now this does not mean in the physical realm only, but also in the spiritual.

Satan is a spiritual serpent, but I want you to know that if the Scriptures are describing a physical serpent, then "in the name of Jesus" you have power over them, too. Mark 16:18 further states, *". . . And if they drink any deadly thing . . . ."* For example, if you should ingest poison (and I dare say that today you take that risk daily in the restaurants you frequent), *". . . it shall not hurt [you]."* I am not saying that you may not feel some effects, but based on the promise in Mark 16:18, *"they shall lay hands on the sick, and they shall recover."* When your brother in the Lord lays hands on you, in faith, and calls forth the poison in Jesus' name to come out from you, you shall be raised up.

Who is this Word given to? To those who believe! Scripture does not say that it is given to the apostles only; it says it is given to those who believe! Now believing does not merely mean that you know Jesus died, that He is up in heaven, and that someday you are going there. Believing means that those things spoken of in the Holy Scriptures are true because Jesus said so. You are to believe in everything without any doubt, with all your heart. No other proof is needed; His Word is enough. Christ himself spoke these Scriptures. Why do we have so much trouble believing when Jesus spoke them and lived them?

Devils consider the body of the person they indwell as their home. In the spirit they are disembodied. They need a body to reside in on this earth in order to accomplish their job: the end result of which is our death. The human body becomes the house, an encasing for the devil.

In Matthew 12:43–45 Jesus says, *"Truly I speak unto you, when the unclean spirit is gone out of a man, he walks through dry places seeking rest, and finding none. Then he says, 'I will return into my house from whence I came out.' And when he is come, he finds it empty, swept, and put in order. Then he goes in, and takes with him seven other spirits more wicked than he is, and they enter in and dwell there; and the last state of the man is worse than the first. Even so shall it be also unto this wicked generation."* Notice in this Scripture that the devil did not say he was going back to the man's house. The devil said he was going back to *his* house. His purpose is to steal, to destroy, and to kill the man.[6]

Where in the body do they dwell? They do not dwell in your spirit. If you have sincerely committed your life to Christ, your spirit is subject to divine influence. *Your soul* is your emotional life, vexed by generational sin, fleshly lusts, evil influence and ignorance, and your own desires and delight in evil. Devils do not dwell in a man's spirit. Devils are spirit. If your spirit has not been subject to the Holy Spirit, then devil spirits can take over and completely possess you. An example of this is a person with a reprobate[7] mind, who malfunctions both mentally and physically. However, if a person has sincerely said yes to Christ unto true repentance, miraculously the spirit of that person is connected with the Holy Spirit of God and the seed of Christ is planted in his heart. Then a process of new birth begins in his spirit.

This new birth process also begins the restoration of the person's soul. Psalm 23:3 says, *"He restoreth my soul; he leadeth me in paths of righteousness for His name's sake."* Since the fall of man our souls have been in death, because we were born in spiritual death through the sin of Adam. This is our human inheritance—our Adamic sin nature. It is your soul which must be saved from this inherited death of the original Adam sin. James 5:19–20 states, *"Brethren, if any of you do err from the truth, and one convert him, Let him know that he which converteth the sinner from the error of his way shall save a soul from death, and shall hide a multitude of sin."* The soul is the vehicle of the heart and mind.

In the natural and unredeemed state, your life is guided by *your* feelings, *your* emotions, and *your* human reasoning. This is why you need redemption. It is unwise for the redeemed to be moved by what he feels. Rather, he should be guided by the Word of God. We all know from experience that we cannot trust our feelings. The reason for this is that we have been and can still be deceived by our feelings through sin by Satan's deceptions.

Most of us were born into families that didn't have all wisdom and knowledge of the Word of God. If they did, they would have been able to entrust His word to us. The extent to which they had the knowledge of God is the exact degree to which they gave it to us. It is obvious, for this reason and the witness of our pain, that we need to receive our Savior. Like our forefathers, we have all come short of the glory of God.[8]

We know that our feelings cannot be trusted. What can be trusted is the *Word of God* as it is revealed by the Holy Spirit, because this living Word renews our minds and protects us from deception. This can be done only through the truth, which is the Word. This basic trust is why the world in its courts of law utilizes the practice of swearing in a witness with a Bible, which is swearing on the *Word of God*. For they acknowledge the Word of God as their only basis for truth. We know that Jesus Christ was and is the Word made flesh, and that He dwelt with us on earth.[9]

The renewed mind is synonymous with the renewed soul. Ephesians 4:23 says, *"And be renewed in the spirit of your mind."* A renewed mind has the mind of Christ: a mind that is at peace; a mind that is right and sound, not a mind that is distorted, tired, haughty, hostile, or reprobate. How do we obtain this mind of Christ? We acquire it through His Word. The more we study His Word through the leading of the Holy Spirit, the more our minds will become like His.

A carnal mind is a mind that dwells on worldly or fleshy things. It is a sick mind. It thinks all kinds of defeating thoughts, such as unworthiness, as well as thoughts of sexual and monetary pleasure. His is a mind receiving its directions from the unholy spirit, Satan. The carnal mind is always in deception; it is puffed up, thinking it knows truth and is intelligent, when it is only in deception and cannot understand the truth.[10] Most of the world has a carnal mind. They do not know truth because they do not have the mind of Christ, yet they think they know everything. We can simply watch television and see this occurring all the time, day in and day out. We can see it where we work and everywhere we go, and, all too often, we can see it in ourselves. I am amazed to see how truly deceived we can become at times. It astonishes me to see what people will agree to or with when they are in deception.

Let us look at the outcome of the natural, unredeemed man. Each and every one of us can acknowledge the fact that we do not know what is going to happen to us in the future. The only thing we have available to us is what someone has told us about a particular situation. If we have not experienced it with our natural minds, we can either accept the information or reject it based upon how it is presented to us. When it comes right down to it, the only thing we can hold to as being absolute truth is what we have experienced through the leading of the Holy Spirit as confirmed by the Word of God.

So we, as humans, have this situation wherein we are influenced by two spiritual entities. The first is God, who created all things for the benefit of man. Every good gift and every perfect gift is from God and is given to us through the wisdom and knowledge of the Holy Spirit. However, contrary to God is another spiritual entity called Satan, who has resolved to do one thing: to deceive you into a position of destruction. Satan's one goal is to destroy you, and his only method is through well-concealed lies that look so much like truths.

If you are in your natural mind and are not seeking redemption and knowledge from God, you are obviously going to receive information from the other source. Self-will exercises two choices: if it is not from God, it will come from the father of all lies, Satan. As I stated earlier, we all can see this situation so plainly throughout the world. We experience this in our own lives when *we lie*. Satan will penetrate man's mind with evil thoughts in order that he might destroy man.

We must be convinced that Satan is the great counterfeiter and that he can counterfeit only what is true. Of course, we must also know that Satan desires to be worshipped, and he must come as close to the truth as possible in order to deceive us without being recognized. Satan would be too obvious if he came to us and said, "Worship me. I will give you your desires if you will make a covenant with me." Most of us would be very fearful to make that kind of agreement. Satan is not interested in the people of the world. He is already their father, and he has already made converts and entered into a covenant with them. For as the Word says, "You cannot serve two masters; you will love one and hate the other..."[11]

Satan is interested in people who have a personal relationship with their Father God through Christ Jesus, because

22

they are the true Christians and the children of light. If we are true believers of Christ, we must bring this all-piercing light to the peoples of the world and the places of Satanic darkness, revealing his sinister plans of deception and destruction.

Satan will try to stop the truth from going forth. This is the reason that he must come to us looking very much like the righteous (angel of light).[12] His tactics of deception must be carried out so cleverly and with such cunning that mere human reason and thought cannot see the difference. No man, without the power of the Holy Spirit (through the gifts given to man by the Holy Spirit), can discern the light from the deception of Satan's darkness. Most of what is discussed concerning Satanic cults and the like is cleverly used to get our eyes off the real dangers.

The true threat is the spirit of Satan operating through what we term "the Church," many times disguised as great religious leaders or pastors, alleged prophets, miracle workers, and teachers of the Word. Such people are being used knowingly or unknowingly for the purpose of deceiving the people. This is the real danger.

Let us look at the life of Jim Jones. As many of you know, Jim Jones had a Pentecostal background and apparently believed in the baptism of the Holy Spirit and the gifts of the Holy Spirit. He was ordained through a well-known denomination and apparently did good work through his ministry in Indianapolis, Indiana. Visibly, he did lots of good work, and many who said they were Christians agreed. It was told that he helped the lowly and down-trodden and did much work within the black and minority communities. To the natural eye it appeared that everything he did was directed by Jesus.

We can now see with our natural eye how deceptive the works of Jim Jones were. Also, we know now that the real work of Jim Jones, as led by Satan, destroyed the lives of *many* unsuspecting and undiscerning men, women, and children. What eventually took place in South America through Jim Jones became clearly visible. Yet today we are watching thousands, hundreds of thousands, and millions being deceived and misled in our churches because of the many ministers that are self-appointed professionals rather than God-appointed and ordained. These men and women are false prophets, wolves in sheep's clothing, hirelings.

A church the size of Jim Jones's did not erupt overnight. It was a working of Satan over a period of time. This is a visible warning to us that we must be very alert through the discernment of spirits as given by the Holy Spirit. Do you have the baptism of the Holy Spirit?

Let me specify that it does not matter what denomination you belong to, for we, individually, are the only Church God has established. And we must find out whether or not we have any deception in us. If we do, we must be quick to rid ourselves of the lies and turn to the truth, because He is coming for a Church without spot or wrinkle. He is coming for the person without spot or wrinkle who claims Him as his Savior. This is why my husband and I, as ministers of God's Word, have struggled so hard to continue to raise a standard of perfection through the washing of the Word of God,[13] so that Christ may present to Himself a glorious Church, one that is undefiled.[14] However, we cannot be deceived and believe that we can do whatever we want just because we once walked up to an altar, raised our hands, and said, "Yes, Jesus,

I receive You into my heart." We must also become Christ-like in our actions and repent from all sin as it is revealed to us. Jesus is coming for a bride, His Church, which is without spot or wrinkle (sin). That bride, that Church, represents you. To my knowledge, nowhere in the Word is it a custom for the husband to prepare for the bride before marriage; it is the bride who must prepare herself for marriage—it is her responsibility.

The Holy Spirit has been given unto us to help and enable us to prepare properly for His coming, so that He may find us without sin, without spot or wrinkle. This is the only time He has said He will return for His bride. Then Jesus Christ will be our husband. But if we want to receive Him, we must be prepared.[15]

Jesus has completed the initial work; there is nothing more for Him to do. He has fulfilled the promise. He has laid all of the foundation for the marriage in preparation for us to go forth and overcome sin. He gave His life for His bride on the cross for the redemption of all who will come to the cross. So we must go forth, get ourselves ready, and clean ourselves by the washing of His precious blood and the cleansing of the Word of God. This will then present, through our obedience, a bride without spot or wrinkle.

Today we do not hear the washing and cleansing part of our walk preached enough from the pulpit in truth and power. However, that does not make it any less an absolute necessity for the Bride to prepare herself for the Marriage. For much too long we have been given—and, frankly, we have sought after—those things that tickle our ears, not that which would enable us to overcome. We must hear the meat of the Word—and it is a tough Word, but one with great power—when we are given it, and receive it through the revelation of the Holy Spirit.

As you know, in the book of Revelation we are told that there will be but a remnant who will enter into the Marriage feast with the Lamb of God. The question must be asked, "Do you want to be counted among this remnant?" This is serious business. This is work! The Scriptures do not teach us that everything will be done for us. We have the responsibility to prepare for the Marriage. Our Lord will not have a Church that is in bed with the world; otherwise, He would be joining Himself to a harlot, and this He cannot do.

Your soul must be redeemed! Hebrews 10:39 says, *"But we are not of them that draw back into destruction, but we are going to be of them that believe to the saving of the soul."* The soul must be redeemed, saved from demon activity. You may have heard from the pulpit that the spirit must be saved. We just read in the Scriptures that it is not the spirit but it is the soul which must be saved. *". . . Believe to the saving of your soul."*

We must be careful what teaching we receive. It is our responsibility, as stewards of our minds, to judge everything spoken in the name of the Lord through the Scriptures. I Thessalonians 5:23 tells us, *"And the very God of peace sanctify you wholly; and I pray God your whole spirit and soul and body be preserved blameless unto the coming of our Lord Jesus."* The whole person must be redeemed; the spirit first, then the soul, and finally the body (a new body, which is granted to us in the resurrection). This is another area of study in itself.

Again, what is the function of our spirit? Our spirit must submit to the Holy Spirit and be governed by the Holy Spirit by our willful choice. When we, by our will, allow the Holy

Spirit to be the indwelling controller, we begin the regeneration of our soul. A "spirited horse," for example, shows signs of hyperactivity and rebellion, because it has a will of its own. And unless it is brought into useful submission, it is without value. In the same manner, our will and our spirit should be subject to the will and the Spirit of God, through Christ Jesus, to the salvation of our soul.

The soul is the real battleground between the Holy Spirit and the unholy spirit, Satan. This is why both spirits can be present at the same time in a believer. I am laying out this rather intensive format for you so that you can see how these unholy spirits (devils) can be at work in a Christian's soul. I hope that through this explanation you will understand *why* and *how* devils are attaching themselves to the unsuspecting and uninformed souls of many Christians.

I believe this book will help you to understand and to gain knowledge, so that you will be able to drive out the unlawful intruders. First, we must have a true foundation so that our understanding of what our spirit and our soul are will be complete, and so that we may understand demonic activity and the obvious presence of demons in so many people today. Later, I will be giving instructions from the Word on how to cast them out.

It is in the interest of Satan and his angels to keep us in a fallen state of existence through deception and darkness caused by a lack of knowledge, regardless of whether or not we have received Jesus by the profession of our mouth. It is in the interest of the devils working for Satan to keep that dark, fallen existence active in our soul. For as the believer becomes knowledgeable of the devices of Satan, he will become more and more united with the Lord of Glory, and thus more able to drive back the forces of darkness of the Evil Spirit.

The true believer becomes equipped through the baptism of the Holy Spirit to recognize these evil spirits and to successfully war against them. This active warfare takes place in the soul of the believer.

It is true that we are not *actually* the children of Satan, but the fall was the result of believing the lies of Satan. Satan succeeded in his deception and thereby entered into the life of the fallen man. And because of the fall corruption runs through every element of fallen man's being. But praise God, when a man is redeemed—purchased through the very life-blood of Jesus Christ—he is translated out of the power of darkness and sin and into the power of the kingdom of God. Every portion of his being actually becomes renewed, stage by stage, through deliverance. Thus he is delivered from the power of darkness and sin which held him captive through demonic activity in his soul. This is a working-out process, a learning process. Philippians 2:12 exhorts, "... *Work out your salvation with fear and trembling.*" Our souls must be consecrated unto God and made whole, delivered step by step, as we, the true believers, work out our salvation through knowledge and understanding of the Word of God.

Notes for Chapter One

[1] Vex:(a) to irritate; annoy; provoke. (b) to torment; trouble; worry. (c) to dispute or make subject to dispute.

[2] 1 Peter 1:18–19

[3] John 10:10

[4] 1 Corinthians 6:20

[5] Hebrews 13:4

[6] John 10:10

[7] In the original Greek, *reprobate* means "unapproved, rejected, worthless."

[8] Romans 3:23

[9] John 1:14

[10] Colossians 2:18

[11] Luke 16:13

[12] 2 Corinthians 11:14

[13] Ephesians 5:26

[14] Ephesians 5:27

[15] Revelation 21:2

CHAPTER TWO

SPIRITUAL WARFARE

(DEVILS ARE OUR SPIRITUAL ENEMIES)

C hurch, please hear me: Devils are the spiritual enemies of the body of Christ; it is our responsibility to deal with them. Remember what is written in Ephesians 6:12: *"For our struggle is not against flesh and blood, but against the rulers, against the powers, against the world forces of this darkness, against the spiritual forces of wickedness in the heavenly places."* As the Holy Spirit said through Paul in Ephesians, the way we wage this warfare is through the Spirit.

Our job is to learn how to wage the war and fight the good fight, as Paul instructed Timothy. (See II Timothy 4:7.)

Again, as a reminder of what was said in chapter one, the word *possessed* in the Greek does not mean total ownership; it means "exercised or vexed by a devil (demon)." We must also remember that a devil indwelling a believer is an illegal trespasser; he is an alien taking residence by unlawful means.

31

As explained in chapter one, we have been purchased with the dear price that Christ paid on the cross by the shedding of His blood. It is, however, up to the Christian *now* to *demand his rights* because Jesus Christ paid the price. A devil cannot reside within a Christian if he *knows his rights* and commands the alien to depart from his property "in the name of Jesus." This takes faith in the authority—*our legal rights*—which has been given to us in Christ Jesus, and faith to believe in the power of His Name.

We must realize that the devil will consider the body of a person his house, his earthly home, *if* he is allowed in and the Christian does not cast him out. Now remember, these devils will wander through dry places after they have been cast out, seeking whom they can enter into. If they find an unsuspecting and uninformed Christian with a door left open through sin, they will enter in. As Jesus said in Matthew 12:43-45, *"Now when the unclean spirit [the devil] goes out of a man, it passes through waterless places, seeking rest, and does not find it. Then it says, 'I will return to my house from which I came'; and when it comes, it finds it unoccupied [not filled with the Holy Spirit and not informed of its* legal rights*], swept [clean], and put in order [religious, but ignorant of the Word]. Then it [the devil] goes, and takes along with it seven other spirits more wicked than itself, and they go in and live there; and the last state of that man becomes worse than the first."* Jesus finishes by reminding us, *". . . That is the way it will also be with this evil generation."*

We must not only know our legal rights in casting out the unwanted spirits, but we must continue to keep ourselves in a state of alert preparedness to keep the intruders out of our dominion. As you know, Jesus Christ had no sin in Him, and the Word says that when Satan came, he could find nothing (no sin) in Him. The Evil Spirit could not trespass on this Holy Ground because Jesus was without sin and knew His legal rights. Jesus said in John 8:28, ". . . *I do nothing on My own initiative, but I speak these things as the Father taught Me.*" We would do well if we would follow the same rule. So on this holy and prepared ground of Jesus, the evil spirits could not trespass. Neither can they trespass upon you, if you are prepared.

You must know that these evil spirits (devils) do not hover around the Christian, but they seek to enter into the soul realm and take up residence within the Christian who has left an opening through sin. Remember, they are spirit, and they will go and connect themselves anywhere they have a legal right, by our permission through sin. As I have mentioned, this concept of hovering spirits is not true and cannot be found in the Scriptures. We can all agree that Satan can do a more devastating job from the inside than he can by having his devil spirits just hang around or hover about.

The soul realm is the part of you in which the sin of Adam is manifested. Your spirit is that part of you which needs to be first renewed and made right.[1] Your soul is that part of you which needs to be restored, saved, and delivered.[2] For a deeper understanding of the functions of your spirit and soul, I suggest that you review chapter one again.

Regarding devils (evil spirits), the first thing we must understand is that all devils are liars and deceivers. They cannot be trusted in anything; the truth is not in them. If we could grab one of these evil beings in our hands and ring it out like a dish cloth, we would not find one drop of truth in it. This is something to meditate on. Think about it: they are so separated from God that they have nothing of value, nothing of goodness, nothing of truth. Is it any wonder that Jesus mostly referred to them as unclean spirits? I can think of nothing that would be more unclean than entities without anything of God in them. Can you think of anything worse to touch, let alone to allow to reside within you? Yet millions of Christians, out of ignorance, are doing just that this very moment. We must be keenly aware of their nature if we are going to successfully engage and defeat them on the battleground of spiritual warfare and cast them out into dry places.

In the following chapters, I will instruct you from the Word on key ways to stop Satan's attacks, and how to defeat him every time—not just some of the time, but every time— and to stop him from ever stealing from you again. We must, however, first remember and never forget that he and his devils will most often come as angels of light or in some form that we have been deceived into believing is not devil activity but some natural phenomenon, such as a virus, bacteria, epidemic, lifestyle, or something other than what it truly is—demonic warfare on man.

If you desire a ministry in deliverance (and you had best desire one if you intend to follow after Jesus and take up your cross, as He instructs in Matthew 10:38), then you must become strong, knowing the instruction of our Lord through His Word, so that Satan will not be able to trick and deceive you. You must be alert and know that, as Jesus warned us in Mark 13:22, ". . . *false Christs and false prophets will arise, and will show signs and wonders, in order, if possible, to lead the elect astray.*"

Something you will begin to learn is that many Christians do not want to get rid of indwelling evil spirits, or they will tell you that they are not ready. You will find that they are either embarrassed (a spirit of pride) and do not want to admit their problems (generally because of some so-called position of importance or authority in a church body), though they desperately need help. Or they are afraid (a spirit of fear) that someone may find out that they have an evil spirit and need deliverance.

Of course, we must also never forget the abominable teaching that good Christians cannot have evil spirits. Others have excused their "problems" as some "natural thing." They believe that if they did not have afflictions they would not be as God intended them. God help us! Unfortunately, you will find these elements in so-called Christians much too often.

The most diabolical outcome of all, however, is seen in those who have walked in agreement with evil spirits for so long that the spirits have become an inherent part of their personalities and characters. These people are not aware that they have devils and therefore have no desire to change. This is the most difficult kind of situation to deal with, because the person only vaguely realizes his plight, and you must work very hard to bring him to a point of agreement.

We must hurry and be about our Father's business. Satan has some of our brothers and sisters in such a state of deception that they are becoming comfortable with their afflictions. Now *that* is true deception. We must also realize, of course, that this is Satan's greatest deception of the Church today: his ability to make us think that God is doing the afflicting and that it is His will to do so. And there are many who think,

"That's life!" If Satan can continue to make people believe that he is not interested in residing within them, he will continue his plunder and pillage of the Christian body.

We must have great compassion and realize that it is difficult to discern the indwelling spirits, knowing that they are liars and masters of deception. Only through the gift of discernment (as given by the Holy Spirit to those who have received the baptism of the Holy Spirit) will we be able to discern the actual indwelling spirits. Therefore, it is only through this recognition of a spirit that you will be able to address the devil and order him out of his hiding place—the soul of the uninformed, sinning Christian.

We all have a definite way of examining ourselves as to whether or not we are having problems with a trespasser. Go before the Lord with anything you feel uncomfortable with, or that you have earnestly tried on several occasions to avoid doing but found yourself unsuccessful and plagued by torment over a long period of time. Under these circumstances you will find that this trespasser has succeeded in becoming a stumbling block in your walk with the Lord. You will also find you cannot get relief when you pray to the Lord about your problem, and you have cried out to the Lord with all your heart, but seemingly to no avail. You have said privately, "Lord, remove this thing from me." "Lord, help me to overcome this thing." " Lord, help me to improve." "Lord, I want to be better." "Lord, if it be your will . . ." If you find yourself fighting this endless battle with little or no success, you have very good indications that someone has invaded your will and is putting you in a state of confusion, and you are bound. You are now in a state of double-mindedness. James 1:7–8 says, *"For let not that man expect that he will receive anything from the Lord, being a double-minded man, unstable in all his ways."*

I have seen so many Christians in this state of bondage seek freedom through their own understanding. They stumble, dividing the Word incorrectly, "always learning and never able to come to the knowledge of the truth."[3] In their frustration they seek counsel and advice from uninformed pastors or Christian counselors. Beloved, I have witnessed many Christian brothers and sisters trying to find answers alone or from uninstructed sources. So many of them have just given up, assuming that God is interested only in the so-called big things. Or they have just walked away totally disenchanted and disillusioned. This is tragic, considering that the answers are so clear in God's Word and that they can bring deliverance when taught properly by a God-appointed and ordained teacher of the Scriptures.

My dear brothers and sisters, if you find yourself in bondage, praise be to God. You know and have the understanding that you are bound by the spirit of Satan through the working of his devils. This is the first step in becoming free—knowing your enemy. Before you can be set free, you must know how and by whom you are bound: Satan's demonic host.

To briefly summarize, if you continue to be oppressed and depressed, even though you read the Word, pray, and seek seemingly good counsel, *you need deliverance!* Let's call to mind the words of Jesus in John 8:32: *"And you shall know the truth, and the truth shall make you free."* Also His beautiful promise in Isaiah 42:7: *"To open blind eyes, to bring out prison-*

ers from the dungeon, and those who dwell in darkness from the prison."

Through God's ministry we have seen Christians who need deliverance daily. Deliverance from Satan ranks second in importance only to people's need to receive the knowledge of Jesus Christ unto salvation. I say this because so often we see dear children of God who profess faith in our Lord Jesus, yet continue to live lives of slavery to sin through demon oppression. Often they cannot believe they need deliverance because they think that devils cannot indwell Christians. They believe they're suffering merely from predestined bad habits or inherited traits. Though I agree that bad habits and inherited traits exist, I have learned that we can get rid of them faster and easier when we cast out the devils that are holding us in bondage to those habits and inherited traits.

If we are honest with ourselves, I'm certain most of us will find areas which have plagued us over and over again. We have tried to overcome these problems time and time again, but to no avail. The reason we have not overcome them is that we have not attacked the real problem. There is bondage in the Christian body, and the reason for this bondage exists is that demon spirits are in control, because of poor counsel.

We have two choices to consider in obtaining freedom from demonic oppression: First, we must become knowledgeable and learn to resist the devil ourselves. Second, a more successful method of ridding oneself of indwelling devils is to seek out a brother or sister who is knowledgeable in the area of deliverance. Deliverance is the process of being emancipated from the suppression and oppression of a destroying force within us. This is possible only if we have come, with a truly repentant heart, to a knowledge that Jesus Christ is our Lord and Savior. Remember, Satan could find no sin in Jesus; we must seek after the same holiness.

If you find yourself in a position where you are trying to live the way Jesus instructed and demonstrated, but you are bound and find it impossible to succeed, it is because of a lack of knowledge. As long as the believer walks in the natural and remains in self-inflicted bondage, he will be no match for the cunning of Satan. This is why the devil does not want this message to go out to the Christian body at large and be put into practice.

In Ephesians 6:10 we read, *"Last of all I want to remind you that your strength must come from the Lord's mighty power within you" (The Living Bible)*. Isn't it amazing that it reads not *our* power, but *His power in us*! When the all-consuming power of Jesus is in you, I guarantee that no power of Satan can long endure. However, you must put on the whole armor of God, so that you will be able to stand against all of Satan's deceptive strategies and multitude of tricks. Be sure to study again and again the verses of Scripture that are given to us in Ephesians 6:10–18. Study them until the words become a part of you, as armor is to a warrior in combat, because, beloved, you are in a real life-and-death combat.

So many Christians are trying to outsmart the devil in their natural minds. Through their physical strength they are trying to stop the advances of Satan. Beloved, there is not enough strength in the natural mind to stop Satan. The only way to stop him is through the strength and power of the Holy Spirit—through the supernatural, through the authority of the name of our Lord Jesus Christ.

One of the first things Jesus instructed us to do in His name was to cast out devils.[4] The key is to be fully knowledgeable, fully aware of our authority as believers and as adopted sons of God through Jesus. John 14:13–14 says, *"And whatsoever ye shall ask in My name, that will I do, that the Father may be glorified in the Son. If you ask anything in My Name, I will do it."* In the original Greek, verse 14 literally means, "Whatever you *demand* in My Name, I will see to it that it is backed up." How about that for absolute authority! You see, we have it! Jesus has promised this to us as children of God, but we must receive it and act upon it. We must stand, knowing that we have the power and the authority through His promise and His righteousness; otherwise, we will be afflicted with mortal and spiritual wounds and never realize the victory was already won for us at Calvary.

If you are righteous because the blood of Christ has cleansed you and because you desire not to practice sin, you will find your authority in the name of Jesus come alive in you through faith, and you will supernaturally know that all the power of Heaven is backing you up. As He said in Mark 16:17, Jesus wants us to be free from the works of the devil in our lives, then spread this good news to others. We know in our heart of hearts that Satan is no match for our Beloved, Jesus. We know that God gave Jesus a name at Calvary that is above every name.[5] But, Church, we must receive this truth through faith—faith in what Jesus has already demonstrated to us in the Scriptures. We know that His ways are infallible.

We must remember that we are not fighting against people made of flesh and blood, but against demonic spirits—spirit beings, spiritual entities without physical bodies. They are real, however, alive and existing in the spirit realm. To say that there is no power in Satan is not speaking the truth. How about his power to deceive? To compare Satan's power with that of Jesus' power is, of course, like comparing night and day. Satan pales in comparison to our Lord. Be aware, in our natural strength we are no match for the deceptive powers of Satan. However, as we move in the knowledge and strength of our Lord by the leading of the Holy Spirit, Satan is no match for us. It was Jesus Who defeated Satan at Calvary, not Satan who defeated Christ. It is Jesus' victory over the devil that gives us victory over the powers of darkness. Praise God! This is not a natural victory, but a supernatural victory.

We are fighting against the powers, against the master spirits who are world rulers of this present darkness, against the spiritual forces of wickedness in the heavenlies (the supernatural sphere). This is the true enemy; this is who we fight. By using the weapons given to us by our Lord, we can resist the enemy whenever and wherever he attacks. And when all the smoke clears, we will be standing!

Devils come in ranks much like our military forces in the natural world. They are well-organized, thousands of times better than man's church today. They know exactly what they are doing and are extremely efficient in their diabolical work. What we do here on earth is an imitation of what already exists in the heavenlies—both for the good and for evil.

I believe man receives his instructions from the holy angels of God and from the unholy angels of Satan through what we term the "*subconscious*" (soul). The unholy spirits—fallen angels—stay in ranks as they did when they were angels of God before the rebellion and fall of Lucifer, after which they were cast out of Heaven. The unholy angels exist today in the dominion of the heavenlies of the earth's realm. These spiritual beings, like their leader, are very cunning. Satan, of course, is their head, and ranking beneath him are the ruling devil spirits. This fact needs to be remembered as we come forth and begin to cast out devils.

You need to discern who the ruling spirits are. They are the ones that have taken control and brought lesser (serving) devils along with them. These ruling devils and their followers are given satanic authority over nations, cities, organizations, churches, and families, and the lesser devils are given authority over individuals. Now they go about their areas of assignment seeking opportunity to destroy. If they can find nothing in you (no sin), they are powerless to enter in and destroy. But if they find sin, this is their open door and they will attack with all boldness and destructiveness, because you have given them the *legal* right through sin. I must repeat this: Only through sin do these spirits, controlled by Satan, have power.

This knowledge must be revealed to the Church. We must know our enemies and the weapons we have to defeat them. Satan has continued to deceive the Church and keep it in darkness; in other words, he has weakened and defeated it. But no longer! Children of God, we are rising up in His strength and driving back the forces that have so long plagued us. It is *past* time that we expose the myths and deceptions of Satan for what they are—powerless lies.

If you will recall, in chapter ten of the book of Daniel, Daniel asked God for an answer to a specific prayer. He was praying for his people, Israel, and he was looking for the release of the captives. He prayed to God, he fasted, and he waited patiently for the answer to his petition. Three weeks transpired before he finally received the message from the angel, Gabriel.

We all remember who the Angel Gabriel is: he is God's chief messenger. (Read Luke 1:26–38 where he announced the birth of our Savior.) As God's messenger, he told Daniel that he had had a difficult time getting through to him. Do you remember why? Gabriel told Daniel that he had had to fight the prince of Persia, who was the spirit commissioned to rule over the country of Persia. He told Daniel that he, Gabriel, had to call for Michael, the Archangel, to do battle against this devil spirit.

From this description you can imagine the condition in which the people of that area must have been. They must have been in great darkness (sin) to be giving this prince spirit of Satan so much power. But as you know the story, Gabriel *did* get through with the answer to Daniel's prayer. God always does answer when we seek Him, which gives us hope for freedom from all opposition. Gabriel explained to Daniel that God had answered his prayers three weeks earlier, but because of the sin of the people the ruling demonic spirit had the power to prevent the message from coming through sooner.

Through the message of Daniel we should be comforted with the knowledge that God has His angels on assignment constantly, working all the time on behalf of His people. We must know that we have multitudes of holy angels working on our behalf. There are many, many more *holy* angels of God working *for* us than Satan has of unholy or fallen angels working against us. God's angels are diligently working and ministering to those who are the heirs of salvation through the saving blood of Jesus Christ.

Isn't that wonderful? This is good news! It should be a great delight to our hearts. We should rejoice continually and thank Jesus for having His angels work in such wondrous ways for us. Paul and I have received numerous reports of miraculous things happening to our brothers and sisters in the faith, reports that can be attributed only to the work of God's angels. They are watching over you right now. Isn't it a wonderful feeling to know that right now there are beings with that kind of power looking out for your benefit! Can we question the infinite love of our Father?!

We also know that angels can appear in human form. Do you recall the incident in Genesis of the three angels who talked with Abraham about Sodom and Gomorrah?[6] Two of these angels in human form went to Sodom and Gomorrah and were insulted by the deviates of those cities when homosexual advances were made toward them. There is little doubt that these angels appeared in the image of man. Of course, their insults mattered little to the angels of God, because with the power vested in them by God they could at any time have wiped away the meager power of Satan. As you know, once they removed Lot and his immediate family from Sodom according to the will of God, they obliterated the sinful inhabitants of Sodom and Gomorrah from the face of the earth. The Scriptures tell us, *"Do not neglect to show hospitality to strangers, for by this some have entertained angels"*[7] without knowing it. Just be very sure you know which kind of angel you are welcoming—holy or unholy.

As God's Church, we have, for the most part, remained in total ignorance. It seems as if no one wants to talk about this vital knowledge. Many of us have casually acknowledged that one third of all angels created by God fell with Satan. Many of us believe that their avowed purpose is to deceive and destroy the body of Christ on earth. And many of us know that the Father has ordained with His power two-thirds of all the angels he created to protect us twenty-four hours a day. I suspect that if we knew on any given day the number of fiery flames of hell shot at us by the fallen angels of Satan, and the number of times those fiery darts were extinguished by the angels of God, we would all be in a greater state of praise to our Father than we are at present. Each one of us can recall numerous times we have escaped from difficulty and truly did not know how we escaped. I suggest we look to God and say, "Thank you, Father, for Your loving care through Your angels."

Can you now visualize the spiritual realm? Can you see these billions, possibly trillions, of spiritual beings—the angels of God—working for you? These obedient beings move and act according to the Word of God. So if we say, "In the name of Jesus, I call forth protection . . ." (over a certain situation), the angels go to work immediately, carrying forth your command through Jesus to its conclusion in accordance with the Word of God.

Therefore, our job is to proclaim the promises of God that we have received through His Word. Then the angels will go forth and work on our behalf. It behooves us to watch what we say. We must speak only God's promises, rather than doubt and fear of Satan's deceptions. Of course, this will take extensive retraining of our soul realm. As we receive knowledge through this study and begin applying ourselves by putting God's Word into action, our victory march into life will truly begin.

Now if you have a situation or problem at home, at work, or within your relationships that persists in plaguing you, you will find an evil agent at work, a devil assigned to that particular situation. Be especially aware of this and consider it only as a temporary stumbling block that must be removed. Remember, the devil spirits have been purposely assigned to hold you back from wholeness of life.

As mentioned earlier, we have been warned that Satan comes to steal, kill, and destroy. He will steal whatever you allow him through your sinfulness. If you permit Satan, he will steal your joy, your emotions, your finances, and your health. He will destroy your physical body through sickness, disease, or any misfortune. This unholy being is angry with you; he will deceive you into accepting death to come upon you. (See Revelation 12.)

Remember, death is an enemy of man. When Adam and Eve were put in the Garden, they did not know death. But when Satan deceived them into sin, death was the outcome of their sin. *"For as in Adam all die, so also in Christ all shall be made alive."*[8] Death is the enemy of man. Do not mistake death as a release from the torment and anguish of this life/world. When you become so distraught because of the working of devils in your life and cannot take any more—that, my friends, is death's process and the fulfilling of Satan's desire for man.

If Satan can trespass *illegally* on your "blood-purchased territory,"[9] he will. And he does not care about legalities or God's law. He will do whatever Christians give him the *right* to do. This is the point being stressed in this book. Satan is a serious offender of our rights. It is his sole business to destroy. Remember that you are fighting a deadly enemy in a deadly war! Do not fight with your flesh, but with the spiritual weapons that have been given to you by God.

Please understand, it is not each other that we are fighting. **We have no excuse for becoming angry with each other,** because no one person is better than another. We have all been deceived. **Girded with this truth, we must direct our warfare against the evil spirits that are activating the strife between us.** We must always reflect and search our hearts and, as brothers and sisters in Christ, forgive one another, especially those we believe have offended us the most. Unforgiveness is the work of Satan and his agents to keep us apart. Unforgiveness is not instituted by man, but by Satan for man's destruction.

The only way to unlock the prison door of our hearts is through forgiveness. Forgiveness is a choice, regardless of what our feelings may be telling us. We must make a willful choice to forgive. We must forgive others who have sinned against us, or God will not forgive our sins against Him.[10] Consider this carefully.

Let me pose an interesting question: Can we afford not to forgive? It is absolutely essential that we be cleansed of all unforgiveness when we go forth to war against the powers of darkness. Otherwise, we will become open targets for Satan's attacks. The authority that believers have in the name of Jesus comes through our true salvation, but the power comes through the baptism of the Holy Spirit.[11]

Many uninformed Christians continually petition God for His help. This in itself is not wrong; God wants to talk with us. But I must say this: all that we need from God has already been provided through the shed blood of Jesus, at the cross, for the redemption of our sins and through the power of His Word. This is directed through the revelation of His Holy Spirit. We simply must receive the truth and act upon it.

Jesus is sitting at the right hand of the Father, seeing that all who come to the Father through Him will receive the promises of God. Beloved, that has already taken place! When we learn how to fight spiritual warfare, we become God's militant church—the overcomers! We finally become the warriors that God called us to be. He has been preparing His army for two thousand years. It is now in the final stages of preparation as the Holy Spirit pours forth the truth of the Word in all power, with knowledge and wisdom, and as we receive it and act on it.

Until now we have not fully understood what it takes to become this foretold army of God. Satan is a beaten foe, defeated by the blood of Christ at the cross. Yet the question is asked, "How come he is so active if he is a defeated foe?" The answer is that we, the Body of Christ on earth, have not yet learned how to use the spiritual weapons of God's arsenal individually and collectively.

Satan was put to judgment long ago when he acted illegally against Christ at the cross, but our part in that judgment is to *execute the judgment* as instructed. Joshua was told to take the promised land and, although he was promised victory, the people of Israel still had to war against their enemies. Who is it that has deceived us into thinking it is any different for us today? But we have something Joshua and the people of that time did not have: the guidance and the power of the Holy Spirit of God!

Notes for Chapter Two

[1] Psalm 51:10

[2] Psalm 23:3; Hebrews 10:39; Psalm 17:13

[3] 2 Timothy 3:7 (NKJ)

[4] Mark 16:17

[5] Ephesians 1:21

[6] Genesis18 and19

[7] Hebrews 13:2

[8] 1 Corinthians 15:22

[9] See Chapter 1

[10] Luke 6:37; Matthew 18:21–22; Luke 17:34; Ephesians 4:32

[11] Mark 11:22–26

CHAPTER THREE

PULLING DOWN
THE STRONGHOLDS

(WALKING IN OUR AUTHORITY)

Jesus explained His ability to cast out devils in these words: *"But if I with the finger of God cast out devils, no doubt the kingdom of God has come upon you."*[1] In this Scripture, the word *finger* translated from the Greek means "power"—the power of God. When you cast out devils, it will not be accomplished by *your* power. But, in fact, it will be brought forth from the power of God's kingdom, which is within the knowledgeable believer. This power is granted to us by His kingdom being established within us: God's power, His might, His finger—not yours. *". . . For apart from Me, you could do nothing."*[2]

Luke 11:21–22 reads, *"When a strong man, fully armed, guards his own house, his possessions are safe; but when someone stronger attacks and overpowers him, he takes away the armor in which the man trusted, and divides up the spoils."* The strong man in verse 21 represents the power of Satan. The stronger man in verse 22 is the power of God in the name of Jesus Christ.

Jesus has overcome Satan and taken all of Satan's armor from him. This is why we can rejoice and marvel in the Scripture, "No weapon formed against you shall prosper . . . "[3] and that *"the weapons we fight with are not the weapons of the world . . . they have divine power to demolish strongholds."*[4] If we can understand I Corinthians 4:20—*"for the kingdom of God is not a matter of talk, but of power"*—we will finally begin to understand a dimension of God and His love for us that would stagger our imaginations.

If you think that the power of casting out devils was given only to Jesus because He is the Son of God, then read Mark 16:17–18 again, which says that the believers "shall cast out devils" and "shall lay hands on the sick and they shall be healed." God has revealed this truth to me. Keep this tucked away in your heart; you will understand why I am diligently working to bring this truth to the Body. This is what God has revealed to me; the more that Christians enter into warfare, the more Satan will suffer loss. I believe that if we all with one voice (by "all" I mean all true believers) said, "Satan, be bound," he would never and could never vex a believer again. Then the angels of God would come forth with a shout and execute judgment for a thousand years upon that old serpent, Satan, binding him according to the Word of God.[5]

What do you imagine would happen if Christians in the unity of the Spirit of God said with one voice, "Satan, you are bound"? This move of the Spirit must become a reality to you

and it must be put into practice with one mind and one ac-
cord. It is the very proof of the power of Almighty God working in us: ". . . *Christ in us, the hope of glory.*"[6] What is that
glory? It is the blind seeing, the lame walking, the sick being
healed, the dead in Christ being raised, and it is us setting the
captives free—not partially free, but totally free. John 8:36
says, "*Whom Christ sets free, is free indeed.*" Satan must be ren-
dered helpless when we command him to be bound "in the
name of Jesus."

"*The thief [Satan] comes only to steal, to kill, and to destroy*"
(John 10:10). When we are hurting, depressed, and oppressed,
who then is at work in our members? Of course, it is Satan at
work through his cohorts. Satan will steal your joy through
lies. He will accuse you of being a failure and tell you that
you cannot be a victorious Christian. You will have false imaginations, confusion will be the order of your day, and fear your
taskmaster. In short, he will render you hopeless. Deception
will make you believe that all of your thoughts are based upon
facts as seen through your natural eye and mind. These ac-
cusing thoughts are not facts, but it is Satan trying to con-
vince you that your salvation has no power.

One of Satan's most common lies relates to sickness and
disease. How does he deceive people? First, he tries to deceive you with some type of symptom, and he has many natural helpers—various medical professionals! But if Satan con-
vinces you through whatever means that you have the symptom of something you have been fearing, then that which
you have feared may come upon you. (Job 3:25) You have
opened the door to infirmity, and Satan is most willing to

enter in through our fears and doubts. Before long your symptoms may become reality.

Most Christians have not been taught how to engage in spiritual warfare. This book has been written to show you, the believer, the answers to who, what, and how to fight the good fight; to train you how to combat in spiritual warfare; and to pull down the strongholds that Satan has so cleverly built up in the lives of Christians.

These strongholds are built up through false imaginations. Think of it, all those areas of life that seem so overwhelming are merely false imaginations, lies from demonic spirits. They are embraced as your own thoughts, when all along they are deceptive lies—strongholds—built up in the mind through Satan's craftiness. Please note that I said "built up." Satan will always seek that unprotected area that is not covered by the truth of God (which is the armor), and he will build upon one lie: *doubt!*

II Corinthians 10:4 tells us, *"For the weapons of our warfare are not physical weapons of flesh and blood, but they are mighty in God for the overthrow and destruction of strongholds."* What God has said is that you are not going to use a physical weapon, but you are going to use the authority already given to you "in the name of Jesus," which is the power you have been given to tear down demonic strongholds.

Now this is what you will tear down: controversies, theories, and human reasoning from all learned sources. It makes no difference where these untruths came from: institutional teaching, great theologians, renowned philosophers and psychologists, your family doctor, your next-door neighbor, or any other proud and lofty thing that sets itself up against the knowledge and truth of God. The Scriptures tell us, "... *And bringing into captivity every thought to the obedience of Christ.*"[7]

The Bible is the inspired Word of God: His knowledge, His wisdom, and His truth. Anything that does not agree with the Word of God, as revealed by the Holy Spirit and confirmed in the harmony of the Scriptures, is a stronghold of Satan. You, my friend, are to tear it down!

For this reason it is necessary to know the Word of God. How else can you know when someone comes to you with some sweet-sounding doctrine or teaching and tells you that it is of God? Or, as is so prevalent today, you may be presented with a Biblical teaching that is humanistic theory cleverly concealed. These teachings always sound so good and are usually oozing with so-called love. And they are intellectually stimulating to the point that one may become puffed up with self-importance, self-reliance, and pride.

For instance, imagine you or someone you know belongs to an organization such as Alcoholics Anonymous, sponsored by your church. You are told that in order to overcome your addiction to alcohol you can never permit yourself to drink an alcoholic beverage, lest you would fall back into temptation and reinforce your predicament. And you must also continue to claim and believe that you are and always will be an alcoholic. You must continually confess your plight before others so that you will always be aware of its influence over you. If you were to believe this theory, then the belief that you are and always will be an alcoholic would become a stronghold in your mind and would control your life.

The purpose of this book is to reveal to you that that which has been erroneously believed to be a disease, addiction, or psychological impairment is in fact demonic bondage. Then the simple step toward ridding oneself of alcoholism would be to bind and cast out the devil of alcohol and any other demonic presence within the person—with his agreement—and set the captive free. Would he then continue to be an alcoholic? Of course the answer is no! He would be free, and any claim of alcoholism would be a lie that would place that person back in bondage.

What God wants is the captives to be free—totally free! Therefore, the stronghold in this example was set in the person's mind by what was believed to be true, but was, in fact, false. This is what the Word of God calls "false imaginations." The only way a stronghold will come down is through the knowledge of the Word of God, and commanding "in the name of Jesus" that it be pulled down. We accomplish this by coming against the lie with boldness.

For instance, if a captive is set free from demonic influence, and he takes a drink of wine at Holy Communion, will it hurt him? Of course not! He is free. The spirit of alcohol and the demonic presence would no longer be in him. Therefore, he is free! John 8:36 is a beautiful Scripture worth repeating: *"For whom Christ sets free, is free indeed."* Look in Galatians 5:1. God says, *"It was for freedom that Christ set us free; therefore, keep standing firm and do not be subject again to a yoke of slavery."*

However, as in the above example, if the person continues to call himself a recovering alcoholic and maintains the word "alcoholic" in his vocabulary; he would be saying that God is a liar, and there would be no deliverance. Do you see how this would be a denial of the power of God to deliver him from the slavery of alcoholism or any other stronghold? In other words, it would appear that the power of darkness is greater than God, and the stronghold would remain. We know this to be a great lie, but many people today in their practices and deeds remain captive to Satan because of the darkness allowed in our churches through a lack of knowledge.

Let's refer to the above example again and illustrate the difference between the works of man and the good news of God. We cannot deny that a person who drinks excessively and abuses himself and others is better off learning how to break his addiction through whatever help man can provide; however, compromising with Satan is not the way of God nor is it in keeping with His instructions to us. We must always maintain the high road and know that there is no need to compromise, because we know that God is more than able to accomplish what He has promised. But when we, as the body of Christ, accommodate compromise, regardless of its nature, we place ourselves in danger of the destruction of Satan; we have moved from the promises of God to the deceptions of Satan. Furthermore, the above example was chosen carefully because it has been upheld as an answer for alcoholics by so many calling themselves believers, when all along it is another trap of our common enemy.

The deception of Satan manifested in a score of other programs within our churches today could be mentioned. They cover everything from psychology to positive thinking, but to name them all and explain the twisted road they travel would take another seven chapters. However, I will wrap up this point with a brief statement that other programs are further illustrations of the subtle way in which the devil deceives us into believing something less than the truth of God. Consequently, we have difficulty accepting God's promises and His power to accomplish His Word.

Now let us continue to take a look at the demonic forces around us and their activity. We need to first realize that demonic activity in its present state of frenzy will only increase in direct proportion to the increase in drug and alcohol abuse, pornography, deterioration of the music and entertainment industry (whether by television, movies, videos, books, or magazines). The standards have been lowered in every area of our lives: from our decaying public schools to the greed of businesses and workers seeking only paychecks instead of excellence in their labors, to the filth and corruption of our governmental agencies.

With all that surrounds us, we know that people are the vessels used by Satan to bring forth these abominations. We must also realize that this will continue to worsen until the minds of unredeemed men are completely darkened and corrupt. We have been told in the Scriptures that in these latter days there will be great distress, unequaled from the beginning of the world until now, and never to be equaled again.[8] We also know that God is pouring forth His Holy Spirit and calling His remnant into action through His Word. "... *When the enemy [Satan] comes in like a flood, the spirit of the Lord shall lift up a standard against him.*"[9] We are God's standard! The word *standard* in Hebrew means "put to flight; make to flee." The Scriptures tell us to "... *resist the devil and he will flee from you.*"[10] We resist him by casting him out whenever and wherever we find him, by the authority invested in us through the shed blood of Christ and by His Name!

Let us take a close look at this authority granted us through the shed blood of Christ and the protection it provides the believers. Ephesians 6:10–18 reads, *"Finally, be strong in the Lord and in His mighty power. Put on the full armor of God, so that you can take your stand against the devil's schemes. For our struggle is not against flesh and blood, but against the rulers, against the authorities, against the powers of this dark world, and against the spiritual forces of evil in the heavenly realms. Therefore, put on the full armor of God, so that when the day of evil comes, you may be able to stand your ground, and after you have done everything, to stand. Stand firm then, with the belt of truth around your waist, with the breastplate of righteousness in place, and with your feet fitted with the readiness that comes from the gospel of peace. In addition to all this, take up the shield of faith with which you can extinguish all the flaming arrows of the evil one. Take the helmet of salvation and the sword of the Spirit, which is the Word of God."* Read and re-read these powerful instructions of God until they are as much a part of you as your heartbeat. Now, these are our protective weapons. Have no doubt that our protection far surpasses any weapons of Satan and his demonic host. Take note that God gives us only offensive weapons: ones used to go forth, always attacking, always taking the battle from the enemy in victory.

An essential weapon is pleading the blood of Jesus over the person under attack from the spirits of darkness. The demonic presence must retreat under the authority of the pleading of the shed blood, because it is the blood that restores man from the destructive works of Satan. The sword of the Spirit (which is the Word of God), is living, powerful, sharper than any two-edged sword, and penetrates to the dividing line of the breath of life (our soul) and our immortal spirit. Your weapons of combat to war against Satan and his devils are the authority of the shed blood of Christ coupled with the Word of God—knowing the Scriptures and applying them to the areas which Satan is trying to destroy.

You see, we do not have to guess what and how we are to fight the good fight. We have a perfect example before us, Jesus, and we must do as He instructs us. Remember when the devil took Jesus to a high mountain and tried to tempt Jesus into worshipping him? Jesus countered the temptation with a Scripture from the book of Deuteronomy and, of course, the devil departed. Satan cannot stand against the truth. Jesus has shown us the way. We need not be defeated! Our Lord and King has left no stone unturned so we can be overcomers. Praise be to His Name!

It is of utmost importance that you know the depth, the width, the height, and the breadth of the Scriptures, not through head knowledge, but through the revelation of the Holy Spirit. Through no other way will you be able to stand. Let me add, if you use any words other than those from the Scriptures at the moment of attack, you will not only lose the battle, but you will continue to lose many battles with Satan until you grasp and apply the truth. Then and only then will the lessons be learned. You must stand firm on the Scriptures. They are not to be toyed with or manipulated into something that fits one's fancy. They must be taken at face value. One cannot improve on the truth, upon perfection. Besides, they are the only weapons that will work in pulling down the strongholds of darkness. His Word is true and His truth has almighty power. We cannot add to that. Praise be to His name!

Before I go any further, allow me to reiterate something expressed in chapter one that must be clearly understood by the Church in general. Remember what Paul the Apostle said by the Holy Spirit in Romans 1:16, *"For I am not ashamed of the gospel of Christ; for it is the power of God unto salvation to every one that believes . . . ."* I believe, for the most part, that a social gospel has gone forth into the mission fields of this country and all over the world. Church buildings, hospitals, and schools are being constructed, and other social and humanitarian programs are being established, such as youth groups, women's missions, homes for the needy, food programs, and the like, which are good in themselves. But, *they are not the Gospel!* This may come as a shock to some, but these institutions and programs do not reflect the Gospel of the kingdom of God as preached by Jesus and the early church, which was truth followed by signs and wonders. The kingdom Jesus proclaimed was at hand. I ask you, Where are the signs and wonders of God being performed through the believers today? Why are venereal diseases, heart failures, and such the order of our times instead of the promise in Isaiah 53:5, which says, *". . . By His stripes we are healed,"* and which was fulfilled by Jesus in 1 Peter 2:24?

We know that the Gospel taught, preached, and lived by Christ was to go forth and heal the sick, cure diseases, cast out devils, and raise the dead, preaching that men should repent and turn from their wicked ways. This is the good news—that He has provided us with the ability to live life without spot or blemish, without compromise, and without retreating to some watered-down lifestyle of partial survival. We are not only to preach repentance, but also forgiveness, with the power of the applied Word of God that sets men free from Satan's bondage. Hallelujah!

After reading chapters one and two about casting out devils, I hope you now understand and are convinced that a Christian can be plagued by a demonic presence within his soul. Furthermore, we are to acquire the knowledge of how to fight the good fight with the power and authority given to us "in His name." Ignorance is only an invitation for Satan to inflict punishment upon us and torment us; the fact that you are a Christian does not exempt you from these unlawful attacks and the following afflictions.

Common Symptoms: Let us now closely examine the pattern of common symptoms inflicted by these indwelling spirits of darkness.

Emotional problems: People who are in need of deliverance will have continual recurrences of the spirits of hatred, anger, fear, rejection (a feeling of being unwanted and unloved), self-pity, jealousy, envy, selfishness, unforgiveness, guilt, condemnation, depression, worry, inferiority, and insecurity. I will later explain that all of these devil spirits bring with them lesser spirits which are under order to kill and destroy.

Mental problems: What we call mental problems are, in reality, an attack of the demonic spirits of mental torment, procrastination, indecision, compromise, double-mindedness, confusion, doubt, irrationalism, insanity, and/or loss of memory.

Tongue problems (uncontrolled use of the tongue): These include lying, cursing, blasphemy, criticism, mockery, railing, gossip, and negative comments.

Sexual problems: These are always patterned after recurring unclean thoughts and acts regarding sex. They include fantasies, dwelling on the erotic, masturbation, lust, perversion, anal and oral sex, homosexuality, sodomy, fornication, adultery, incest, provocativeness, seduction, and harlotry.

Addictions: The most common addictive spirits are nicotine, alcohol, various types of natural and synthetic drugs, so-called medications, caffeine, and foods.

Physical infirmities: Diseases and sicknesses inflicted on people are called infirmities in the Bible. When a devil of any disease and sickness is cast out, you need to pray for healing of the damage and the restoration to.a healthy body.

Religious error: Objects or devices such as crystals, pyramids, and idolatrous statues attract devils into dwellings and, of course, to the dwellings' occupants. Common sources of error are documented as follows:

1. False religions. Eastern religions, pagan religions, philosophies, mind sciences, yoga, eastern exercises, and self-defense techniques, such as karate. (No matter how much people try to disguise these, they still cannot be divorced from the heathen worship of false gods.)

2. Christian Cults. Mormonism, Jehovah's Witness, Christian Science, Rosicrucianism, Theosophy, Unity or Unitarian, and others. These cults deny or confuse the necessity of Christ's blood in the atonement of sin.

3. Cults. Many so-called lodges such as Free Masons, societies, and social agencies which use religion (Scripture and even God) as their foundation but, of course, omit the blood atonement of Jesus Christ. These types of cults are classified as "bloodless religions."

4. Occult and Spiritism. Seances, witchcraft, magic, Ouija boards, levitations, palmistry, handwriting analysis, automatic

handwriting, ESP, hypnosis, horoscopes, astrology, divination, channeling, etc. Any procedure that seeks supernatural knowledge, wisdom, guidance, and power apart from Almighty God is forbidden to the Christian, because doing so brings a person into agreement with Satan. Occult devils are the most deadly to the spirit of man.

5. False Doctrines. 1 Timothy 4:1 warns of an increase in doctrinal errors. They are promoted by deceiving and seducing spirits. They are designed to distract Christians from the true moving of the Spirit, as well as to bring division and cause confusion in the Church. A compulsion to be obsessed with a certain doctrine espoused by a group or denomination—such as "once saved always saved" or "praying the dead out of a state of purgatory" and many other false doctrines found in religious denominations—incites the person receiving the error to be unteachable. A common flaw of these groups is to put emphasis on fleshy and social activities as a means to the spiritual.

If you have questioned yourself as to whether the common symptoms mentioned above stem from spiritual or psychological problems, I will demonstrate through Scripture that they are in fact spiritual first and prove that the term "psychological" is a false concept due to error. *The error is in the practice of treating the psyche (mind) and neglecting the person's spirit.* Let us concur, then, that man is spirit, mind, and body. The Bible tells us, *"If we live in the Spirit, let us also walk in the Spirit."*[11] Notice it does not say, "If we live in the mind, let us also walk in the mind."

To establish the truth that man's afflictions are spiritual and not psychological, let us take a look at the good spiritual fruit as described in Galatians 5:22–23. In this "List of the Fruits of the Spirit," you will see that the first fruit of the Holy Spirit is *love*; second is *joy*; third is *peace*; fourth is *patience*; fifth is *kindness*; sixth is *goodness*; seventh is *faithfulness*; eighth is *gentleness*; and ninth is *self-control*.

Opposite the fruits of the Holy Spirit you will find the corresponding fruits, or ruling spirits of the unholy spirit. First, you will see *hate* as the opposite of love, love being holy and hate unholy. Second, *mourning* is the opposite of joy, joy being holy and mourning unholy. Third, *strife* is the opposite of peace, peace being holy and strife unholy. Fourth, *impatience* is the opposite of patience, patience being holy and impatience unholy. Fifth, *brutality* is the opposite of kindness, kindness being holy and brutality unholy. Sixth, *evil* is the opposite of goodness, goodness being holy and evil unholy. Seventh, *doubt* is the opposite of faithfulness, faithfulness being holy and doubt unholy. Eighth, *roughness* is the opposite of gentleness, gentleness being holy and roughness unholy. Ninth, *rebellion* is the opposite of self-control, self-control being holy and rebellion unholy. These are the nine fruits or ruling spirits of the unholy spirit.

With each of the ruling spirits of Satan, beginning with hate, you will find the following lesser or accompanying spirits that are linked with and under the command of the ruling spirit. For instance, the *spirit of hate* is the spirit ruling over the spirits of mourning, strife, impatience, brutality, evil, doubt, roughness, and rebellion. Then under these there is another order of lesser spirits. With the *spirit of mourning* you will always find the spirits of depression, sorrow, grief, sadness, and despair. The ruling *spirit of strife* will bring with it turmoil, conflict, anger, confusion, and bitterness. The *spirit of impatience* will always bring with it the lesser spirits of irritability, frustration, intolerance, anxiousness, and temper. The *spirit of brutality* will be accompanied by the spirits of ruthlessness, meanness, savagery, and viciousness. With the controlling *spirit of evil*, you will find the spirits of pride, wickedness, depravity, jealousy, and murder. The *spirit of doubt* will bring with it the spirits of unbelief, distrust, fear, and suspicion (lack of confidence). The *spirit of roughness* will bring with it the spirit of coarseness, pitilessnes, vulgarity, crudeness, and abuse. The *spirit of rebellion* will be accompanied by the spirits of lust, filth, greed, gluttony, drugs, and alcohol.

As you can see, the negative characteristics mentioned above, which are labeled *common symptoms*, are not psychological in nature, they are spiritual.

The fruits of the Spirit should then be evident in our lives. It will be either one or the other—holy or unholy. We will either be walking in agreement with God or with Satan; there is no in between state.

List of the Fruits of the Spirit

Fruits of Holy Spirit	Fruits of Unholy Spirit
1. Love	1. **Hate** (Mourning, Strife, Impatience, Brutality, Evil, Doubt, Roughness, Rebellion)
2. Joy	2. **Mourning** (Depression, Sorrow, Grief, Despair)
3. Peace	3. **Strife** (Turmoil, Conflict, Anger, Bitterness, Confusion)
4. Patience	4. **Impatience** (Irritability, Frustration, Intolerance, Anxiety, Temper)
5. Kindness	5. **Brutality** (Ruthlessness, Meanness, Savagery, Viciousness)

6. Goodness	6. **Evil**
	(Pride, Wickedness, Depravity, Jealousy, Murder)
7. Faithfulness	7. **Doubt**
	(Unbelief, Distrust, Fear, Suspicion)
8. Gentleness	8. **Roughness**
	(Coarseness, Pitilessness, Vulgarity, Crudeness, Abuse)
9. Self-control	9. **Rebellion**
	(Lust, Filth, Greed, Gluttony, Drugs, Alcohol)

Notes for Chapter Three

[1] Luke 11:20
[2] John 15:5
[3] Isaiah 54:17
[4] II Corinthians 10:4
[5] Revelation 20:1–2
[6] Colossians 1:27
[7] II Corinthians 10:5
[8] Matthew 24:21
[9] Isaiah 59:19
[10] James 4:7
[11] Galatians 5:25

CHAPTER FOUR

DISCERNING THE SPIRITS

(PREPARATION FOR DELIVERANCE)

As we learned in the previous chapters, the word *bondage*, when translated from the Greek, means, "a controlling entity or force outside of yourself." When a person is in bondage to something, that thing becomes a false god. Let me expound on this by saying that when a person is in bondage to a devil, that devil is a controlling force within the person and has established itself as a false and controlling god over him. That person becomes its slave. He will be obliged to pay homage to the controlling entity until the false god is overthrown. Therefore, your personal will is overpowered and under the control of a demonic enslavement. This demonic presence is making decisions and causing you to act as it wills. This will continue until the trespasser is cast out.

As you will recall, in chapter three we listed the fruits of the Holy Spirit on one side of the page and the bitter fruits of the unholy spirit on the other side. Please study this list over and over so that you will know and understand these spiritual forces with your mind (human reasoning), as well as discern them in your spirit. This preparation will allow you to be used by God to free those who are afflicted.

We also discussed the various ruling spirits under Satan's command and the lesser devils who act under the authority of the ruling devils. We covered some of the most common symptoms found in those who are more visibly afflicted, such as mental disorders and abnormalities. This chapter will focus on the actual instructions of the ministry of deliverance and how you can be used as a vessel of God to set the captives free.

Before we begin, let us be sure of the foundation in our hearts: (1) You must belong to Jesus without compromise and without reservations; and (2) you must believe in the power of God as given by the Holy Spirit. Now with the gifts of the Holy Spirit and the authority granted to you in the name of Jesus, you are a vessel ready to be used by your Father.

Do not take these foundational requirements too lightly. Avoiding the necessary preparation for deliverance may result in adverse consequences, as seen in the account of the Jewish exorcists in the Acts 19:13–17. As pointed out in earlier chapters, we, in our natural flesh, are no match for the deceptions of Satan. We must have our feet well-grounded in our faith in Christ, and permit the Holy Spirit to use us for the common good of the Church. *Heed this warning: Do not think this is some religious exercise! It is, without question, a struggle against the powers of darkness, whose primary purpose is to come into the Christian's life to steal, kill, and destroy.*

Now, let us continue with the actual application of this work. When people seeking help present themselves to you, most of them will not be totally aware that the help they are seeking is spiritual in nature. Most often they will think their problems stem from persecution by others or a variety of other reasons. Their awareness is dulled by their senses, yet they are desiring help. You should first be aware that the person was sent to you by the Holy Spirit and that the Spirit of God is preparing the person's heart to receive His precious gift of freedom. However, you must also be aware that the person will be influenced by two spirits: first, the Holy Spirit, Whose purpose is to free the slave; and second, the unholy spirit, whose design is to keep the person enslaved.

Preparation for Deliverance

Bring yourself and the person needing deliverance into agreement with God by evoking the name of Jesus over the proceedings. Ask for His guidance and protection, knowing that the demonic spirits are all liars and boasters, full of pride and threats. Be always watchful and discerning lest at any time they attempt to deceive you.

Encourage the person to be honest about all aspects of his sin life and about generational sin. (See Exodus 20:5.) You should first lead the person to repent from his sin and search his heart for unforgiveness toward God or anyone who has offended him. By listening to the Holy Spirit you will be able to discern if the person has truly repented and has decided to forgive and be liberated from the entrapment of sin.

Any sin not confessed and repented of will only keep the person under legal captivity to Satan, and Satan will continue to act upon his legal right. In other words, when one who continues in sin is in direct agreement with Satan, he remains in rebellion to the authority of Almighty God. Psalm 32:5 says, *"Then I acknowledged my sin to you and did not cover up my iniquity. I said, 'I will confess my transgressions to the Lord'— and you forgave the guilt of my sin."*

Do you know what the trouble is with man? He is guilty! Do you know why man suffers as a result of sin? No matter how hard man tries to be a free thinker, without the accountability to the Word of God he is guilty. Because of ignorance and failure to seek instructions from God, he fails and suffers from the guilt of sin. He is in agreement with Satan. Of course, *Satan then attacks the person legally because of his sin, bringing death to the spirit of man, confusion to his mind, and afflictions to his body.* But Jesus Christ went to the cross to take away our guilt! Hallelujah!

Everyone of us has been guilty, and everyone of us has suffered from our guilt because of our sin. We all know that guilt has been a tormenting factor in our lives. To the degree that you give up your sin is the same degree to which you will receive freedom from bondage. As you can see, the spirit of guilt wants to remain in what it claims as its house. Why? Because it has a legal right, through sin, to remain. *Furthermore, guilt is the outcome of unconfessed sin and, of course, sickness and disease are the outcome of sin manifested through guilt.* A person may try to cover guilt through various fleshy ways, such as drugs, alcohol, and other human diversions. However, guilt will always remain. How then does one get rid of this tormentor? We just read in the Psalms: Confess your sins to the One who can forgive them— Almighty God.

What About Psychologists?

Now, many attempts may be made to get relief through psychologists, but a *psychologist cannot forgive sin*. They cannot even offer comfort. Therefore, the practice of psychology cannot relieve anyone's guilt. It is amazing how many supposedly intelligent people spend small fortunes and extensive amounts of time going to someone who, in reality, can do nothing to release the torment of sin. The psychologist can, at best, only appease the person's senses through the recommended use of antidepressant drugs, which is only a temporary and delusive procedure that prolongs the torment. What he needed all along was to take his sins to Jesus and ask for forgiveness.

God has set in His Church a governing body called the fivefold ministry among the general assembly of the Church. These of the fivefold ministry consist of apostles, prophets, evangelists, pastors, and teachers. God's word stresses that these gifted men and women who have earned certain status, with conditions, are given to the body of the Church to perfect the saints, God's children. The word "perfect" is translated in the Greek as: mature, complete, perfect.

In the New Testament there is no mention of learning institutes provided or available for the education of these divine gifts. The Bible speaks of no expectation of scholarly degrees or classes of psychology for the application of this ministry. No, on the contrary, it is based solely on the work of the Holy Spirit upon God's chosen and His anointed vessels.

Let me preface by saying this: God can and will use anything at HIS disposal to meet us where we are. At one time in the Old Testament He used a donkey to rebuke and bring forth a warning (see Numbers 22:22–32). However, this is not God's best intentions for mankind.

To further this point, I present two issues:

1.   There is not mention in the Bible of a practice of hanging a shingle over one's door to give credence to one's ability or right to change hourly wages for God's gifts of love and deliverance.

To me this is an abusive practice to the work of God. At it's very best. I am not saying that a workman is not worthy of his wages, but I am saying that a gift of love (be it money or otherwise) would be more suitable or fitting, as led by the Holy Spirit.

2.   The Church has leaned too often on "well-intended" Christian counselors or Christian psychologists to do the work of a Pastor, who is the sub-shepherd under christians. He willingly lays his life down for the sheep.

Also, it should be noted that schools of psychology teach that the mind (psyche) is to be analyzed to be helped. Although it may be difficult for some to understand this, the psychoses is not the problem of the mind but of the human spirit. Schools of psychology are unlearned in the realms of the Spirit, therefore the TRUE explanation for man's emotional and mental condition has gone unnoticed. The presence of evil spirits as mentioned in previous chapters and man's inborn guilt is his foremost and original problem and enemy. He could only be saved through the blood of Jesus Christ by receiving His forgiveness.

Because the church for the most part has been conditioned by the reasoning of the worlds psychologist and because of the importance of the subject matter, I will once again reiterate what has been mentioned in previous chapters. Let me preface by saying that it is quite possible that one could be helped by a Christian psychologist, if in fact God's redemptive plan and purpose is delivered to the patient with true discernment, lead by the Holy Spirit. In this case, the psychologist or counselor would be operating or functioning more in the capacity of a Minister of God rather than a professional. This practice would make him a HIRELING. The Bible has much to say about this undertaking. As said, in the book of John, an hourly wage charged for spiritual or so called mental help is considered a hireling. The Apostle, by the Holy Spirit, spoke unquestionably against one who does not rule rightfully God's sheep. *A hired man tends the sheep for money, while the shepherd does it for love. This does not indicate, nor necessarily suggest that the well-intended psychologist or counselor working on his case does not love the patient. But by it's implication, it affirms that the shepherd (Pastor) mentioned in the scriptures, is committed to his sheep to love them to the significance of undeniably laying down his life for the flock that God has given him. A professional psychologist or counselor, most likely will not have this commitment. If I could, with the validity of the Spirit, convict you of this standing, then we with the wisdom of God, will begin to assist the Church back into her rightfully intended position.

There is no doubt as we are searching for God in His fullness, that He is in control of every situation we face and allows people to cross our path at a point in time which would guide us to the light. However, the perfect is to seek God's anointed through His government for the lasting result of victory.

*John 10:12–13

You may ask, "If all we need to do is ask for forgiveness, why would anyone need deliverance from devils? Would not the devils flee in the presence of repentance?" The answer is that, although it is true that the forgiveness from sin brings supernatural relief and peace to the believer, the person must take action and repent—a complete turning away—if he would stay in that state of holiness. Although the desire may be there, this is not always an easy task. Therefore, deliverance from evil spirits is sometimes a necessary action and should be seriously considered and gratefully welcomed. When you begin to minister deliverance, you will see the reality of devil spirits, and you will witness many manifestations of illegal trespassing.

Deliverance takes total dependence on God. We must be totally submitted and humbled before Him to properly minister deliverance and to maintain the faith to see it through.

Now the manner in which to successfully administer deliverance is to resist Satan. As stated earlier, this takes total dependence on God. If you will recall from chapter three, it is with the power of God that you cast out devils—not your power, but the power that comes from the kingdom of the living Lord within you. The person needing deliverance must have faith that he can be delivered, and he must have confidence in the deliverance minister.

Paul and I have learned that those most willing to be delivered have had the greatest success in being set free. The individuals who were willing to put down their pride and their carnal concepts were able to loose the lesser devils from their hiding places and allow the ruling spirits to be revealed. This made it possible to demand the departure of the devils by invoking the name of Jesus, and it made it impossible for them to remain.

Before going any further, it is important that you establish in your heart the fact that the person ministering the deliverance must be a righteous individual, one of faith, with an attitude of prayer, and without any unforgiven sin. Satan will recognize the power of Christ within the deliverance minister. As I mentioned earlier, an account of such a lack of righteousness is recorded in Acts 19, beginning with verse 13. It says, *"Some Jews who went around driving out evil spirits and tried to invoke the name of the Lord Jesus over those who were demon-possessed. [Remember the word possessed here comes from the Greek word meaning "vexed with a demon.] They would say, 'In the name of Jesus, whom Paul preaches, I command you to come out.' Seven sons of Sceva, a Jewish chief priest [notice this was a chief priest, a very learned religious figure of that time], were doing this [alleged deliverance]. One day the evil spirit answered them, 'Jesus I know, and I know about Paul, but who are you?' Then the man who had the evil spirit jumped on them and overpowered them all. He gave them such a beating that they ran out of his house naked and bleeding."* My friends, be forewarned, something of this nature will happen to anyone who encounters devils and commands devils to come out without the authority of the kingdom of God firmly established .

There are churches today toying with deliverance ministries as part of their fellowships' outreach to the community. Some, possibly many, do so without understanding its seriousness and what is required of its people. This could be very dangerous for the uninformed but zealous Christian worker. In Acts 19:17 we read that when the beating of the seven men and the Jewish priest became known in the city of Ephesus to both Greeks and Jews, they were all seized with fear and the name of the Lord Jesus was held in high honor.

What is happening in the Church world today is that the name of Jesus is not being held high, because the Church is not moving by the power of the Spirit in the kingdom of God. Verse 18 says, *"Many of those who believed now came and openly confessed their evil deeds."* Praise God, for that is what we must see in the world today—the manifestation of God's power and evidence of His everlasting love in action by the casting out of devils from His people.

Acts 19:19 goes on to say, *"A number who had practiced sorcery brought their scrolls together and burned them publicly. When they calculated the value of the scrolls, the total came to [over $22,000]. The word of the Lord, then, spread widely and grew in power."* Wouldn't you like to see that happen today, especially considering all the occult material being distributed in book stores throughout the world? We must recognize this as the power of Satan ruling over the people involved in the "New Age Movement."

Friends, do not be surprised if the person coming for deliverance has the strange compulsion to turn from your door and flee. The evil spirits are very aware of what is going to take place and that they are about to lose their self-proclaimed home. Remember, the demonic spirits will know if you are real or just trying to build up a ministry and reputation without a clean heart before God. When the Holy Spirit is within you, the devils know they are coming before the presence of God, not you. They recognize the Holy Spirit within you.

Procedure for Deliverance

1. Plan ahead for the deliverance by selecting beforehand a place where there will be no disturbances or distractions. I suggest that windows be closed and all telephones be taken off the hook or disconnected. I recommend that the ministry be conducted by two that are not novices in the ways of deliverance. There can be more people present if they are seasoned Christians who have faith and the ability to continue in prayer and agreement during the deliverance.

2. The blood of Jesus should be pleaded (this means to appeal or entreat earnestly) over the ministers, the person receiving the deliverance, and all others present. In the name of Jesus, plead His blood over the spirits, minds, and bodies of all present, binding Satan from any interference. I sometimes pray in the following way: "Satan, I bind and rebuke you in the name of our Lord Jesus Christ, and by the authority of that name, I now break your power over [the person being delivered]. I plead the blood of Jesus over our spirits, minds, and bodies by the authority granted to me through His shed blood." You should evoke this authority because there is literal power in the name and blood of our Lord Jesus Christ.

3. Encourage the person to make a legal proclamation by his mouth that he wants to be set free.

4. Ask the person to search his heart and see if there is anyone he has not forgiven, for in all cases there is need for forgiveness in past relationships and generally in present relationships as well. No matter who the person has wronged or who he believes has wronged him—whether real or imagined—the need for forgiveness is paramount to the deliverance. Matthew 6:14–15 says, *"For if you forgive men when they sin against you, your heavenly Father will also forgive you. But if you do not forgive their sins, your Father will not forgive your sins."* This is very clear. Without forgiveness there is no deliverance from evil.

Forgiveness is one of the most miraculous gifts God has offered to us. We must know that the cross itself *is* forgiveness, for upon that cross Jesus took away our guilt. It is essential for all deliverances.

It is vital to the deliverance process to have knowledge of and belief in the necessity of using the name of Jesus and of being a vessel of the Holy Spirit. The name of Jesus is the power in which you have been given authority over Satan. Deliverance cannot take place without this all-encompassing name. It is, in fact, your "power of attorney" to act on His behalf. Philippians 2:9–11 says, *"Therefore God exalted Him to the highest place, and gave Him the name that is above every name, that at the name of Jesus every knee should bow, in heaven and on earth, and under the earth, and every tongue confess that Jesus Christ is Lord, to the glory of God the Father."* Upon evoking that name, your authority is granted. Jesus destroyed the works of Satan on the cross and has been given the authority over all things in heaven, on earth, and under the earth.

When you are dealing with Satan's demonic host, there is no other name that can execute judgment upon them. Holding up the crucifix, as you have seen in movies and in some religious pictures, never did and never will get the job done. It is His name and His name alone—not Buddha, not Confucius nor any Hindu god, nor any other "Jesus" but the Jesus of the inspired Word of God—spoken from the mouth of a true believer that will bring forth deliverance from the attacks of Satan. *He is the One Who earned the right upon the cross. He, and only He, died for our sins. He, and only He, has promised resurrection from the dead as the beginning of more to come. He, and only He, conquered death itself.* This is a magnificent word which becomes more and more glorious each time I hear it!

You must believe in His Word and have knowledge of all of His works—and these works should be evident in your life. Hearing is not good enough. James, the half-brother of Jesus, told us through the Holy Spirit in James 1:22–24, *"But prove yourselves doers of the Word, and not merely hearers who delude themselves. For if anyone is a hearer of the Word and not a doer, he is like a man who looks at his natural face in a mirror; for once he has looked at himself and gone away, he has immediately forgotten what kind of person he was."*

The book of Joel speaks of blowing the trumpets and sounding the alarm on His holy hill. (I pray and hope these studies are doing that—blowing the trumpet, sounding the alarm in Zion. "Zion" means among all the Christians.) We are giving a loud and long trumpet call at the direction of Almighty God. Oh, how we hope that it will be heard. Joel 2:32 says, *". . . And everyone who calls on the name of the Lord will be delivered; for on Mount Zion and in Jerusalem there will be those who escape . . . ."* Remember, Zion represents the body of

Christ—the true believers. Jerusalem is a type and shadow from the Old Testament of the Christian body today as it represents the believing Church where there will be deliverance among the survivors.

Unfortunately, not all will be survivors. Some have waxed cold[1] and have fallen away from God's grace. The Scriptures tell us that in these latter days there will be many who will fall out of grace and turn away from the faith. God help them! However, we know that those who receive deliverance from sin will survive. He calls many, but not all come; not all feel worthy of the call. Not all will accept that they are not worthy in themselves to receive this calling, but it is through the worthiness of Christ that we must all come.

In these latter days, the trumpet has been blown . . . we are to go out to battle. Christ has won the battle for us, but it is up to us to fight the war that was started by the fall of Adam—the first man—and finished by the power of the second Adam—the risen Lord of lords and King of kings, Jesus Christ. Satan has been here all along killing, destroying, and stealing from us. Thank God, we have the victory in the second Adam, Jesus Christ, Who has redeemed all that will come by the narrow gate.[2] Those who come by this gate He is in the process of restoring to the glory of the first man He created.

It is my desire to see God's Church walk in such victory that when Satan comes, he will find no sin within us. Praise be unto the name of Jesus, for Satan will not be able to operate with his *filth and lies* in the body of Christ any longer. Instead, you, the overcomer, will be strong and powerful to tear down all strongholds of the devil and thereby establish the kingdom as we are commanded. And you will be His overcoming Church—His pure bride. He will come for those without spot or wrinkle.[3] These are the overcomers. The Spirit speaks clearly to the churches in Revelation 2 and 3, that he who *overcomes* will receive promises and the inheritance of all things of God,[4] including the promise that *God will not blot out our name from the Book of Life*, and only those who have ears to hear will understand.

Would you overlook this essential requirement for becoming an overcomer for salvation? You may ask, "What am I supposed to overcome?" The answer is "sin, Satan, and the world"; not just what you understand breaks the Ten Commandments, but a greater commandment—to abstain from the sins of anxiety, fear, worry, concern, unforgiveness, hatred, and anger. As mentioned in the previous chapters, these so-called emotions are the results of evil spirits operating in Christians today because of their sin of unbelief. I believe that every man and woman desires to be an overcomer. They want to put Satan under their feet.

It is one of the works of the Holy Spirit to come into our lives and enable us to overcome, to make us brand new creatures in Christ. It is a process, a journey, as well as an adventure! It is a working out of your salvation with fear and trembling.[5]

Do not avoid your obligation; see it for what it is—zeal, freedom, life. Anyone who has experienced the enabling power of the Holy Spirit has witnessed less and less sin in his life. Victory is close at hand. Everyone walking this narrow road can readily see that they are practicing sin less now than they did a year ago, and even less than two years ago. We have cause for hope . . . cause to know . . . cause for lasting encouragement. Through Christ we are, in fact, doing as He commanded: becoming perfect[6] as our Father in heaven is perfect.[7]

5. The person must renounce all things that are evil in which he has knowingly allowed himself to be involved. Renunciation is an important part of deliverance. Renunciation means to make a clean break from Satan's works within you.

6. After the person being delivered has renounced all sin, it is important to command the devils in that person to unlink themselves by the authority in the name of Jesus.

Indwelling devils are seldom found alone. They are always in groups. When one devil is discerned, you should immediately look for its companions or lesser devils. A group of devils is seemingly banded together for the purpose of controlling a particular area of the person's life.

In these groupings there will be a "strong man," or ruling spirit. The Holy Spirit will alert you and direct you as to when and how to drive out the ruling spirit. In our experiences, sometimes the Holy Spirit has revealed the ruling spirit first, and other times He has revealed and directed us to drive out the lesser spirits first. You must be sensitive to the Holy Spirit's leading and always leave the deliverance procedure to Him. You must listen and watch carefully, using discernment as your guide. Keep yourself as a vessel under the command of the Holy Spirit. Through experience, I am convinced that the ruling spirits enter a person first, making way for the lesser spirits to come in. In chapter three we learned that all the ruling and lesser spirits have names. When devils are being driven out, you must command the ruling spirit, by name, to come out and take with it its lesser spirits.

There is a tendency among Christians to look for pat formulas. Let me assure you that you had best remain totally dependent on the leading of the Holy Spirit, because in all the years of working in this ministry of deliverance, Paul and I have still been surprised at the cleverness of Satan and his host. Therefore, rely upon the Holy Spirit; follow His leading. If you do not do this and something goes wrong, fear could enter in. Bear in mind that fear has no place in the serious work of deliverance. I have witnessed many different methods of deliverance and I believe we are safer staying as close as possible to the methods used by Jesus and His apostles. They have always been my example. Be careful to never get yourself into bondage through rules and reasons that you formulate. If we see success from using a certain technique as instructed by the Holy Spirit, we are prone to conclude that it was the technique that did the deliverance.

Sometimes the deliverance is done by the laying-on of hands. We have at least two instances in the Scriptures of the laying-on of hands. First is the healing of Peter's mother-in-law in Luke 4:39. We are told that Jesus "rebuked the fever." He treated the fever as a personality. This indicates that the fever was demonic. The parallel account in Matthew 8:15 says, *"And He touched her hand, and the fever left her …*

A second instance of touching or laying hands on a person for deliverance is the case of the woman who was bowed down by a spirit of infirmity. Again we read in Luke 13:11–13, *"And, behold, there was a woman which had a spirit of infirmity eighteen years, and was bowed together, and could in no wise lift up herself. And when Jesus saw her, he called her to him, and said unto her, Woman, thou art loosed from thine infirmity. And he laid hands on her: and immediately she was made straight and glorified God."*

However, the laying-on of hands is not always necessary. Sometimes we simply speak to the devils without touching the person and command them to come out. Then other times we have been led to assist the person during deliverance to cast out of him or her the demonic presence in the name of Jesus.

We have experienced times when the Holy Spirit moved as He willed, leaving us on the sidelines with our mouths open. I was once among a group of praying women and was led to cast out a particular devil of torment from one of them in the group, when to my surprise there was a loud shriek from another woman. The woman was violently thrown to the floor and lay there before me slithering like a snake. I immediately commanded the devils to come out of her and flee from our presence in the name of Jesus. They did, glory to God. But I want you to know, this taught me a powerful lesson. When you are commanding a devil to come out of a person while in the presence of a group, you may be speaking to more than one devil and to more than one situation of demonic trespassing. This has proved to be very helpful to me in understanding what can occur in group meetings.

Now, we must realize that devils can indwell any part of the human body, but one of the favorite areas seems to be the lower abdomen. When a hand is laid on this area in ministry, the devils very often seem to come up and out through the mouth. When hands are to be laid on the abdomen, it is wise and, I believe, helpful to have both a man and a woman involved in the deliverance. A woman can lay hands on women, regardless of the area of the body; and likewise, a man on another man.

Chapter five is an explanation of the manifestations of devils. It is important to emphasize that we are *not* to fear evil spirits. The Bible gives us assurance that we can engage devils in battle with absolute confidence and without fear of retaliation. Luke 10:19 says, *"Behold, I give unto you power to tread serpents and scorpions, and over all the power of the enemy, and nothing shall by any means hurt you."*

Notes for Chapter Four

[1] Matthew 24:12
[2] Matthew 7:13
[3] Ephesians 5:27
[4] Revelation 21:7
[5] Philippians 2:12
[6] The Greek translation of the word *perfect* in Strong's Concordance is *teleios*, which means, "complete, (mental and moral character) completeness; of full age, mature, perfect
[7] Matthew 5:48

Chapter Five

The Deliverance

(Procedure for Deliverance)

To minister deliverance most effectively, you must not only be prepared within yourself spiritually, but you must also have people with you who believe in the power and authority of Jesus' name. Actually, the more believers agreeing together, the better, because agreement in the power of God manifests the power. The Scriptures tell us that if you and the Lord are in agreement, "A thousand shall fall at your left, and ten thousand at your right hand . . . ."[1] We are not talking about *people* falling here, we are talking about demonic spirits (fallen angels). This is a confirmation that we do not fight against flesh and blood, but against the evil powers of darkness.[2] In some people there are just a few devils. If you have a severe case, however, you might find quite a few—sometimes hundreds, depending on the possession.

You should also select an appropriate location to conduct the deliverance. You can go to the home of the person needing the deliverance, or you can conduct deliverances in an open meeting. My husband Paul and I have found that the most convenient place to conduct deliverances is in our own home. Over the years we have lost count of the number of people God has set free while we sat around our kitchen table.

Deliverance requires the absolute moving of the Holy Spirit of God. It should be done in an atmosphere where neither the deliverance ministers nor the person being delivered from devils can be distracted by thoughtless and uninformed people, or by the attempts of the satanic host to distract your faith and hinder the work of the Holy Spirit. So, in short, the environment where the deliverance is taking place should be void of ringing telephones, children attempting to gain attention, animals, and noises from the outside world (as much as is possible). And, most important, have only those present who will stand in absolute faith and intercede in prayer throughout the deliverance procedure. In consideration of neighbors and others who may become frightened or curious, it is best to shut doors and windows, keeping the sounds of prayer and deliverance within.

It is vitally important in preparing for a deliverance to cover with the blood of Jesus the surrounding area and all who are involved. Also, ask the Father in the name of Jesus to send His warring angels to surround the area, commissioning them to hold back any attempt by Satan to reinforce his host of devils.

We normally conduct deliverances around a table, sitting up straight in comfortable chairs. Deliverance is not something you can set a stopwatch to, and many ministers are not aware that this time is not theirs, but the Lords. It is a move of the Holy Spirit.

You will notice tension, nervousness, and sometimes irritability in the person. Express to him or her love, and help him to feel at ease and, as much as possible, at peace. This will alleviate the fear that is prevalent in all people needing deliverance. Many times you will be led to bind the spirit of fear first so that the person can be at ease.

Steps for Deliverance

During the deliverance it will be necessary to write things down, not only to assist your memory, but also to keep a temporary record of these activating spirits and their various ways of interacting and manifesting. Specific steps for ministering deliverance are outlined as follows:

1. Submit yourself unto the Lord in prayer for guidance, and apply the blood of Jesus upon the afflicted as explained in chapter four. Jesus purchased us with the shedding of His blood and destroyed the works of Satan on the cross. This is the victory.

2. Bind all evil spirits. At this point we do not name devils or call them by name, but we bind them *all*, putting bondage on all of them so that they won't have an opportunity to act independently.

As we command the devils to leave, we speak with authority; we say something to this effect: "Devils, I know you're there; you have no right to stay because this person belongs to Jesus Christ. Jesus purchased him/her with His own blood. I bind you and I command you to loose him/her and to let him/her go now, in the name of Jesus." That is somewhat of a format that you would use. It could be changed, however, as the Holy Spirit gives you discernment and direction.

3. Ask the Holy Spirit to reveal the devils, and in particular the ones He wants driven out first.

4. Break generational sin bondage. "*. . . Visiting the iniquity [sins] of the fathers upon the children to the third and fourth generations of those who hate [God].*"[3]

5. Ask the person about relationships, primarily with his or her father and mother. Herein usually lies the key to discerning what demonic spirits you are working against.

6. Pay careful attention to the spirits of rejection, rebellion, and pride. These are ruler spirits who have a whole nest of lesser spirits attached.

When you ask the afflicted person about their relationship with their parents, you will need to seek the Holy Spirit as to what questions should be asked. Remember, it is necessary that the gifts of the Holy Spirit be operating in your life, because you need the gift of discernment and the power to cast out devils. (These gifts are spoken of in Mark 16 and I Corinthians 12). As you ask these questions, the Holy Spirit will begin causing the evil spirits to reveal themselves within the afflicted person.

After you have taken the necessary steps, deliverance will happen easily; however, keep in mind that you must always be flexible, because you do not want to create methods and quench the Holy Spirit. The Holy Spirit must always have free reign.

As explained in previous chapters, we have all been rejected at some point in our lives, some to greater degrees than others and depending on the experiences we have had with our parents, from the womb to the present. I mention the womb because you may not have been wanted in the womb; but you may have been wanted after birth when your parents saw how cute you were. But seriously, quite often a very young woman or an older woman has many deep fears about pregnancy and childbirth and have questions about rearing the child. Often the mother becomes pregnant out of wedlock and brings shame and guilt upon herself. These experiences happen because of the unredeemed life. It is not necessary for mankind to experience these terrible afflictions. They come because of our rebellion against God and His Son.

In other situations the parents' priority was to accumulate wealth. The child was unwanted because he or she was an inconvenience and was conceived before the desired time. The web of selfish ambition entraps the parents, the child is birthed in conflict, and the struggle has an effect upon the unborn child; thus, the spirit of rejection. To the degree that the parents have known and served the Lord will be the same degree (lessor or greater) to which the victim feels rejected. Unless there was guidance, true spirituality, and love, you will find a strong spirit of rejection within the victim.

When you detect this spirit, you will always find the spirit of rebellion as well, rebellion being the original sin of Adam. When a victim has felt rejection because of his rebellious parents, he will also encounter the spirit of fear, resulting in timidity. It is important to note here that the parents have not truly surrendered their lives to Christ; they have made themselves their own gods. These demonic spirits are passed from generation to generation until the victim has an encounter with the cross and receives the Holy Spirit. Only then can this curse be broken with the knowledge that he can be delivered by the power of God.

The fear of rejection will also bring a nest of other unholy spirits such as hurt, anger, and hate. In some cases they may not be noticeable, but in more extreme cases they will be obvious. The spirit of hurt will have taken residence either because of the devastating experience of rejection or because one or both parents prefer one child over another. Ultimately the spirit of rejection will open the door to self-hate, with the subsequent hate of others.

The spirit of pride will always be prevalent in these cases because the victim feels the need to protect himself. One spirit brings in the other, and this is very destructive to the person's soul. We know that pride is the very sin that caused Satan himself to fall, and when you have the spirit of pride, you have the evil one himself.

Mourning, evil, and rebellion are ruler spirits, and lesser spirits such as fear and hurt are under their command. This trinity is found quite often enforcing the spirit of rejection, and it is up to you to take authority over the ruler spirits. These higher powers are talked about in Ephesians 6:12: *"For we wrestle not against flesh and blood, but against principalities, against powers, against the rulers of the darkness of this age, against spiritual hosts of wickedness in the heavenly places."* Once these spirits are bound in the name of Jesus, those that remain will come out quite easily, although not always in that particular order.

7. As we bind Satan and the ruling spirits, it is wise to command the devils to unlink themselves; they are jointly combined in a nest, huddled together. In the name of Jesus *forbid* them to help one another.

As the deliverance is coming to a close, if you feel that all demonic spirits have not been revealed and cast out, command the devils to reveal themselves individually by using your authority in the name of Jesus. Then as they reveal themselves cast them out. For example, if there is a ruling spirit of strife, there could be five other lesser devils, such as the spirits of turmoil, conflict, anger, confusion, and bitterness. Only through the supernatural gift of discernment can we know which spirits are indwelling and if all demons have been dealt with. Don't rush—you are working with a person's life!

Notes for Chapter Five

[1] Psalm 91:7
[2] Ephesians 6:12
[3] Exodus 34:7; Deuteronomy 5:9

CHAPTER SIX

MANIFESTATIONS OF DEVILS

(RECOGNIZING OUR ENEMIES)

During the process of deliverance devils will begin to manifest or show evidence of themselves in various ways. Undoubtedly, the most common manifestation is coughing. The cough may be dry, but sometimes it is accompanied by mucus. In extreme cases, there may be vomiting, spitting, or foaming at the mouth. Other manifestations include crying, screaming, sighing, roaring, and yawning. People who yawn or sigh out their devils are just as delivered as those who have the more violent manifestations.

A rather common manifestation is one that shows itself in the hands. The fingers may become extended and rigid. Arthritic spirits often manifest themselves in the hands. The hands become very stiff and the fingers gnarled. This may happen even in the hands of teenagers and young people who as yet have had no visible indications of arthritis; yet the devil of arthritis is already at work. The devil may also manifest itself by pain and twisting of the body.

An awesome manifestation is that of the *death spirit*. This spirit can be seen on the countenance of the person as a deadness in the eyes. Quite often the person's skin has no vitality and has a feel of lifelessness. The skin of the person takes on the waxen pallor of death. The spirit of the person is depressed, and he may have been involved with or around severe sickness.

Odors are another facet of the manifestation of devils. You may smell an unpleasant odor around the person being delivered.

Devils may cry out with a loud voice. I have heard a piercing demonic scream after the spirit of torment has been cast out. Sometimes this happens when the devil of witchcraft is cast out.

The spirit of pride may manifest itself in several ways. It may cause the person to sit or stand erect and fold his arms across his chest. It may cause him to tilt his head back with his nose high in the air as a haughty gesture. Talking too much and bragging about oneself is another potential manifestation of the spirit of pride. The person finds it difficult to let others speak and will keep interrupting them. They feel that what they have to say is much more important than what others may have to say. Also, the spirit of self-importance will be linked with the spirit of pride. The spirit of pride or self-importance will make a person "*. . . think more highly of himself than he ought to think . . . .*"[1]

Spirits of nervousness and tension may cause pain in the back or neck. During the deliverance, the minister should lay hands on the area of pain and command the devil to relinquish it's hold in the name of Jesus.

Other manifestations that may be witnessed during deliverance ministries include cramps in the legs and arms, nausea, crying, and sometimes laughing. The laughing is often a mocking spirit trying to make light of the ministry. A novice might think that the person being ministered to is lacking in seriousness, but the laughter is entirely separate from the person's own feelings.

Devils speak through their victims. Quite often the novice thinks it is the person speaking, but you will soon learn that it is a devil. At times there is a voice change from a lower to a higher pitch, or vice versa. The minister should not encourage the devils to speak unless there is a specific devil he wants named in order to secure deliverance.

Conversing with devils should not be done unless the Holy Spirit gives you specific instructions to do so. When they speak they may contend that the person wants them there, or they may threaten to come back if they are cast out. At times they plead not to be cast out.

When devil spirits are cast out, they sometimes leave through the mouth or nose. The most common manifestation of this is coughing.

Devils seem to know that the eyes of a person reveal their presence. The victims will most often keep their eyes closed or look away from the minister who is looking at them. I have also seen during a deliverance the victim's eyes take on the look and glare of a serpent.

Devils will usually respond to a description of what they are causing. For instance, "You devil that is causing this person to have bad dreams at night, I command you to come out, in the name of Jesus!" This stradegy is the most simple one when the minister is not aware of the demon's name, and it will then come out. There is value in naming the devils, in that the person being delivered becomes aware of what indwelling devils were cast out in case they try to reenter.

Devils prefer to seek and indwell another human after they have been cast out. If they cannot find a being to dwell in, they will try to enter an animal. It appears that the devils need anything warm-blooded. Nowhere in the Scriptures have I read that Jesus or the apostles cast devils into a pit or hell. The Scriptures convey that the devils were commanded to go to dry places[2] until the appointed time of their execution.

Here are a number of things to note when you begin to minister deliverance:

1. It is extremely time-consuming. Mark 7:24 says, ". . . *He [Jesus] entered into an house, and would have no man know it; but He could not be hid."* If you take this ministry of deliverance seriously, this Scripture will soon become a reality for you.

2. It will be necessary to get as much rest as possible because much of your energy will be used in the warfare against the spirits of darkness. Often Jesus found Himself wanting to get away to rest alone and be with His Father. You must do the same.

3. Your patience (one of the most profound fruits of the Spirit) will be tested. There are those who are slow to learn and do not retain their deliverance, and you will have to repeatedly encourage them. It is always good to remember at

these times that we are only as good as our weakest link, and that the weaker souls among us should be doubly honored.[3]

4. Deliverance will also take a tremendous amount of love, dedication, strong faith, and Scriptural knowledge. Remember that while Jesus was in the wilderness He spoke the Word of God when He rebuked the devil. In it all, there will be an overflowing of God's blessings and rewards, as one by one you see the captives set free from the demonic hold of Satan. There is no greater glory or joy! In the last chapter, instructions will be given on how to help a person keep his deliverance.

5. Sanctification is the ultimate in deliverance from devils. We can compare the devils to airplanes and the old nature to an airport. If we tear up the "landing strip," there won't be any place for the devils to land. If we are dead to lust, how can we have a spirit of lust? Evil spirits attach themselves to the old nature in the soul realm. The Pharisees accused Jesus of performing miracles by Beelzebub. Do you know what "Beelzebub" means? It means "the lord of the flies." What a perfect illustration. Where do flies attach themselves? Not to a spotlessly clean vessel, but to a stinking pile of garbage. Our sin natures are like garbage heaps and they draw flies … they attract devils. The best way to get rid of devils is to get rid of the sin nature.

Notes for Chapter Six

[1] Romans 12:3
[2] Matthew 12:43
[3] I Corinthians 12:22–25

CHAPTER SEVEN

STAYING FREE

(RETAINING YOUR DELIVERANCE)

Once a person has been set free, it is important to keep in mind the following eleven points for retaining the deliverance:

1. You must watch for any negative thoughts. You yourself will have to become like a watchman standing in a watchtower, consistently watching for the attack of the enemy. In this case, you will not be in a watchtower within a walled city, but in the watchtower of your mind. Through redemption you have been given the helmet of salvation as part of your armor.[1] This armor is placed over the mind area. Satan's attacks will be made on your mind and emotions within the soul realm, so that through his devils he may rule you, building up strongholds by inviting other devil entities.

When you have negative thoughts, realize that they are coming from the enemy. The way to combat negative thoughts is with the Holy Scripture. For instance, you might be having a financial problem. You cannot pay your bills and the creditors are calling. Satan comes in like a flood with the reinforcement of fear. Fear will attract anxiety, worry, and concern. The stronghold begins to grow. You, the watchman, need to be awake and aware of the attack upon yourself. You do not want to be caught sleeping and unaware and in a false sense of security. You draw out your sword, as a soldier in combat in the army of the Lord. That sword[2] is called the Word of God. You attack with the Word of God, using a Scripture that befits the problem. An appropriate Scripture would be Philippians 4:19: *"And my God shall provide all your needs according to His riches in glory in Christ Jesus" (emphasis added).* Now the negative thought has been removed and the Scripture which is truthful and positive has taken its place.

2. Another example is reflected in the case of an attack upon your flesh, such as pain in your stomach. Perhaps this pain conjures up thoughts in your mind of an attack of appendicitis, because your mother had that affliction. Even if you do not have appendicitis, the negative thought has entered with the onset of pain, bringing with it fear and other related spirits. And now you have become pretty well convinced.

Do you see how this works? What are you to do now that you have been alerted? You must again draw out your sword to do combat. This time the Scripture will be different, fitting the condition. You're beginning to be trained as a soldier. The Scripture you choose might be I Peter 2:24: *". . . By His stripes you were healed."* This verse denotes that as a result of the atonement and blood sacrifice of Jesus, sickness and disease have been taken upon Himself. Therefore, the provision has already been made for you, and you are "more than a conqueror."[3] Praise God, you do not have to fear. Now you can see how Satan's cohorts work to deceive.

3. Any negative confessions characterize demonic influence. Confess what God's Word says. If you are frustrated because of a certain situation that is out of your control, you might replace it with the Scripture, *"I can do all things through Christ who strengthens me."*[4] Out of your mouth will come either life or death for you, for when you speak righteousness and the Word of God, angels of God go to work on your behalf. When you speak negatively, the evil spirits go to work against you. *"Life and death are in the power of the tongue . . . ."*[5]

4. A person cannot maintain deliverance unless the Word of God is a primary factor in his life. The Word of God must be primary in his life because the Word contains our instructions for life. The Word of God is a lamp to our feet, enabling us to see without stumbling.[6] It shines in the darkness and gives us understanding and knowledge. Nothing can be compared to it.

5. By crucifying the flesh we break all bad habit patterns. Now the breaking of old habits becomes easier. Why? Because you have been delivered from the controlling devils, and their strongholds have been torn down by the work of the Holy Spirit.

6. Continue to praise God for what He has done for you. Praising God becomes natural. It is a confession of what we have received and it is our testimony. We confess it and we tell others. It's great and it's marvelous, and there's nothing like it!

7. Stay in the fellowship of God and your spiritual family, where you will be encouraged, edified, and comforted.[7] If your church does not sufficiently meet this need, seek one that will.

8. Get under the authority of those shepherds who are willing to lay their lives down for the sheep, those who are willing to pour the oil and the wine on the wounded soul.

9. Find and fulfill your function in the body of Christ. This will be accomplished by serious, dedicated prayer.

10. Desire and receive the spiritual gifts spoken of in 1 Corinthians 12. These are the tools for life.

11. Commit your life to Christ. Surrender yourself wholly, keeping your faith and trust in God no matter what your circumstance. Allow the fruits of the Holy Spirit[8] to grow in you. This righteous fruit will fill your house after you have been cleansed. No devil will be able to return when it sees your house sealed with faith, trust, and the fruits of the Holy Spirit. Devils cannot stand goodness. Goodness bothers them so much that they must flee from you.

In I John 4:1–6 John wrote, ". . . *Believe not every spirit . . . .*" He warned that the spirit of antichrist and the spirit of error (deception) were already at work within the church. He instructed them to doubt every doctrine and teaching until they were proven to be of God. We are told to "try the spirits."[9] One good way to discern the true from the false is to look for evidence of the fruits of the Holy Spirit.[10] Also, be aware that Satan will try to slip in and hinder us from being able to discern the fruits by giving a false sense of security.

God put a curse on the serpent and gave him a promise:[11] "*And the Lord God said to the serpent, 'Because thou hast* done this, thou art cursed above all cattle, and above every beast of the field; upon thy belly shalt thou go, and dust shalt thou eat all the days of thy life.' " God said to man, "In the sweat of thy face shalt thou eat bread, till thou return unto the ground, for out of it wast thou taken; for dust thou art, and unto dust shalt thou return."[12] Thus the first Adam, now fallen, is declared to be dust of the earth—earthly, flesh (sin nature). As such, man is the rightful food of the serpent, old Satan. These terms are symbolic and spiritual in regard to Satan. Snakes do not eat dirt, but Satan does prey on the Adamic nature; in other words, the old sinful nature—the flesh.

You may wonder why Satan is allowed to afflict you, tempt you, and/or torment your mind. It is because you are still bearing at least a portion of that image of the first Adam, the man of dust, and the dust is the serpent's food. He has a right to prey on you as long as you have that old dust nature. Starve the serpent by feeding the new man with the Word of God and dying to the flesh—the old nature—and give the serpent little, if anything, to feed on.[13]

Simply put, the devils will attempt to fasten upon some area of the fleshy mind and body, then move in to exercise control over that facet of the *personality*. They will invade when given the opportunity, and they will not leave unless they are resisted or forcibly evicted by the legal authority of the name of Jesus. Left unchecked, they will trespass on people and cause much suffering, misery, and unhappiness.

Matthew 12:43–45 tells us, "When an evil spirit comes out of a man, it goes through arid places, seeking rest, and does not find it. Then it says, 'I will return to the house I left.' When it arrives, it finds the house unoccupied [please pay special attention to the word "unoccupied"], swept clean, and put in order. Then it goes and takes with it seven other spirits more wicked than itself, and they go in and live there. And the final condition of that man is worse than the first . . . ." We are told plainly in these verses that it is possible for a devil to be cast out but then return to a person, bringing with it more wicked spirits, leaving that person in a much worse condition than he was before the devils were cast out. This is a frightening fact.

Therefore, it is very important that the ministers of deliverance have a clear and precise understanding of their responsibilities in not only delivering a person as directed by the Holy Spirit, but also in teaching him how to stay in the protection of Almighty God and how to keep his deliverance. When we consider that death is brought upon us through devil activity within, we begin to understand the importance of getting rid of and staying rid of the devils. Only then will we have the abundant life promised to us by God. The way to receive this abundant life is through knowledge of our Lord Jesus Christ and living His way.

Now that the person has been freed from devil possession, his house is ready to be filled (occupied) with Jesus ("His Spirit"). The person of Jesus is pure; the fruit of the Holy Spirit is His character, and the baptism of the Holy Spirit is His power. *"But you will receive power when the Holy Spirit has come on you . . . ."*[14] Remember, the people in the church spoken of in Acts knew and walked with Jesus for a long time, and one of the things they knew was that they needed His power. The Church today is no different. Many say they know Jesus. Good, then they need to know His power, the Holy Spirit.

Now you can more readily see that there are certain steps that must be taken after a person has been delivered from the demonic presence within. I have heard short routine prayers after deliverance that went something like this: "Now, Lord, fill up the empty places." This type of prayer will actually cause the loss of the deliverance. Why? Because the devils will see the person's ignorance and, of course, return with a vengeance. As I said, I know this is often done out of ignorance and is certainly not intentional. However, it is very serious and very dangerous! We cannot afford ignorance when dealing with the precious commodity of God's gift of life, because, *"My people are destroyed from lack of knowledge."*[15]

For each devil that is cast out, the gifts and fruits of the Holy Spirit must be received in order to replace the demonic presence. When a person has been delivered and has not already received these spiritual gifts, it is essential that he be taught about them and how to receive them. These gifts will endow him with the power to overcome sin and the temptation to sin, thereby closing off the avenue through which the satanic forces may return. The person will then be able to operate effectively within the body of Christ, and be able to witness and to be used in the power and might of our Lord Jesus Christ and His salvation, with signs and wonders following. Glory, hallelujah! What a witness to a dying world . . . freedom with power! We must know that these spiritual gifts of God and their manifestations are given to every man that sincerely seeks; they are to profit the body, to build up and to overcome sin.

These gifts are the nine gifts of the Holy Spirit and are found in I Corinthians 12:8–10. These gifts are for the benefit of the Church, for they are mighty in the pulling down of Satan's strongholds. What a beautiful picture of the weapons given to us as soldiers of the cross and of the power of Christ within us.

Quite often Christians find out that the gifts were hindered from coming forth because there was a need for deliverance. When they are delivered, the gifts begin to flow through them with much greater faith and power.

There is still another aspect of Christ that the person who has received deliverance must be filled with, and it is called the fruits of the Spirit.[16] These fruits must be developed within the believer, and they are developed by the watering of the Word of God through the revealed knowledge of the Holy Spirit. Simply put, it is reading, knowing, and acting upon God's instructions. It is important to note that the fruits of the Spirit are not a free gift, as are the nine gifts of the Baptism of the Holy Spirit. The fruits are earned by the believer's persistence in making correct decisions and choices (accomplished by asking and receiving from the Holy Spirit), then by continuing to abide in righteousness according to the Scripture.

Both the gifts of the Holy Spirit and the fruits of the Holy Spirit—these marvelous characteristics of God—will work in the life of the believer and produce maturity, completeness, and perfection. Through the power of the gifts of the Holy Spirit in operation and the working out of salvation through the maturing of the fruits of the Spirit, the overcoming Christian will keep his eternal deliverance. Don't misunderstand me; the fruit is not produced by any independent action of the believer or by self-effort. We can't produce peace, joy, love, and so on. We might think we can, and we may even try in our own strength, but the end result is always failure. And every time we fail, we suffer from a feeling of unworthiness and low self-esteem.

On the contrary, if you choose to abide in Jesus, the fruits of the Spirit cannot fail to be produced in you. Allow me to repeat this truth: The fruits of the Spirit cannot fail to be produced in you if you choose to abide in Jesus. The ability to produce rather than to fail comes from abiding in the vine (Jesus). The key is to abide! Abiding in the vine means staying connected to the root (Jesus), so that the life of Christ can flow into the branch (the believer) and produce fruit.

How do we abide in Jesus? By keeping His commandments. Scripture teaches us that by abiding in Jesus and keeping His commandments we love God.[17] When we obey His commandments, we abide in Jesus and have fellowship with God; we obtain the fruit of His love, and ultimately His joy and His peace will follow. When we are disobedient, we keep ourselves from the love of God, and Satan has gained a right to enter in. If Satan finds the believer's house filled with the gifts and fruits of the Holy Spirit, he cannot enter in.[18] Praise God, this is where we must be. This is the predestined position of man in the will of God.

In John 15:10 Jesus said, *"If you keep my commandments, you shall abide in my love; even as I have kept my Father's commandments, and abide in His love."* What is being said here is that we are to keep His commandments. And what is His commandment to us? To love the Lord your God with your whole heart, and to love your neighbor as yourself. (See Matthew 22:36–39). In other words, if you truly love with the love of God, you fulfill all the law and all commandments, and you do for others what you would do for yourself.

Jesus said in John 8:28–29, *". . . I do nothing on my own but speak just what the Father has taught me. . . . I always do what pleases him [keep all of His commandments]."* Jesus knew the importance of keeping God's commandments. We also need to understand the paramount importance of keeping God's commandments. We should, as Jesus did, ask God about each decision. We will be amazed at how much He will begin to direct our lives into production and perfect love. It is for this reason that Jesus was able to walk a sinless life. Always keep in mind that He was mortal man, flesh and blood, just like we are, and He faced all of the same temptations.

We are in the latter days and Satan is bringing forth every enforcement of his host of devils. The Scriptures tell us that he knows his days are numbered. This is why drugs and other perversions of every kind are so prevalent today. The Lord showed me in the Spirit that He is starting to close His gate very slowly; soon it will be shut and no man will be able to enter in. (See Matthew 25:10.)

I believe that in these last days God is raising up a mighty army to storm the enemy strongholds and free the captives in the mighty name of Jesus. I believe that we, as well as others, are being raised up for a time such as this to arm the believers with the Word of God and to allow us, by His strength, to help lead the way in the final attack on old Satan. Our ministry of deliverance is a fulfillment of a prophecy given to Paul and I five years before this ministry began. We believe it is a prophecy not just for Paul and I, but for the Church that is awakening to the sound of the trumpet call of God.

The words of prophecy which were spoken over Paul and I through Kerry Bulls in a service on May 16, 1982, at the Faith Center of Escondido read as follows:

"Praise God, you've got a beautiful spirit, both of you. And the Spirit of the Lord would say this unto you: I have called you even as a beautiful candle that would burn on the mantel place of the home, a beautiful home. I have called you as that candle, and you will burn, and you will shine. And that wax that would melt, that would drip down the side, is the anointing of God, that would spill over unto other people. Yes, and the flame that I have called to burn in you as candles of the Lord will ignite other flames, and it shall grow unto a bonfire, saith God. A bonfire of deliverance and salvation. And many things shall happen. The anointing of the evangelist shall rest upon you, even that which is happening in the earth today in a new way. For I am not calling you these things according to traditional concepts, but I am speaking unto you in the concept of what I am doing today. And I have given you a special ability to bring people into the Kingdom. And you shall do it even as those in the early Church operated from day to day as they went about their business, as they went about their business, even those miracles of God happened and as you go about your business, saith the Lord, miracles will happen. The business of the Kingdom will be transacted in your lives. And many people shall stand and say thank you for your ministry. Thank you for being courageous. Thank you for being obedient. I am basking in the love of God because of you. And this is just the beginning. The candle flame is flickering now, but it shall burst into a large flame and consume the work of the enemy. It shall start in Jerusalem and it shall burn to Judea and Samaria. And it shall continue to burn, saith the Lord, for I am starting in your home and in your house. And I am burning away the work of the enemy. And the fire of God is being established in those places."

The following is a *word of instruction* from my husband regarding the deliverance ministry:

"Go into a serious time of intercessory prayer and pray two ways: One, that you will be used mightily by God through His instructions by the Holy Spirit to go forth within this ministry. From what I have viewed within the Body of Christ, I believe that after our salvation, after receiving the free gift that Jesus has offered, it is of paramount importance that we allow ourselves the freedom to grow to the level of maturity we are called to. So I ask you to pray and if ever the following words were true, it is now: The harvest is plentiful, but the workers are few. Two, beseech the Lord of the harvest to send out workers into His harvest. I believe we are now in days that are to be the last moments of this time. We need laborers in the field."

The following is a *word of prophecy* brought forth through my husband regarding the deliverance ministry:

"But I say to you teachers of the Word of God, awake from your religious slumber. You who have been given so much and have been entrusted with such awesome responsibility, your time for accountability is at hand. You who have been charged to lead toward glory have been visiting perdition upon your charges. Awake, open your eyes to the counsel of God. Jesus is the Light upon the mantel. Follow His Way. It has been clearly marked. Look anew upon your anointing. Examine the fruits of your labor. Jesus came so that man could be free. And I have commissioned you to follow after Him. He pointed the Way. Awake, O teachers. Awake!"

Our prayer is that you receive and claim it with us. May God richly bless you!

Notes for Chapter Seven

[1] Ephesians 6:17
[2] Ephesians 6:17
[3] Romans 8:37
[4] Phillipians 4:13
[5] Proverbs 18:21
[6] Psalm 119:104
[7] Hebrews 10:25
[8] Galations 5:22,23
[9] Galatians 1:6–7
[10] Galatians 5:22–23
[11] Genesis 3:14
[12] Genesis 3:19
[13] Romans 8:13; I Thessalonians 5:23; and II Corinthians 7:1
[14] Acts 1:8
[15] Hosea 4:6
[16] Galatians 5:22–23
[17] 1 John 5:2–3
[18] 1 John 5:18

Oh God, how beautiful is your creation. The mountains, trees, grass, and your flowers. You want to take it and bring all inside yourself. You cannot take it all in, for it is all to Splendid. Colors and shadows in a composition of absolute peace-hanging like a three demensional portrait in a soft graceful breeze. The sound of music engulfs me. Man with his ability to perceive takes what was generously and freely given and with tending brings back the garden, yet Eden is not fulfilled until the peace endures within.

In my limited mind and vocabulary I somehow know that love is the essence of what I see. It is eternal, it is endless. Only our own limitations within our soul stops the ever expanding glory that we as man have been granted. We disturb it in our confusion, distressed by fear. All things have been granted, all things are possible with the Spirit of Truth. Man may fly, build, produce unlimited. What marvel, what a gift. Do we understand this power, this magnificence, or do we console ourselves with mundane and the trivial until there is nothing left for us to imagine. Our comprehension becomes nil until all that can be felt and experienced is death. From such doom we have been delivered, from such a destiny we've been saved. Opportunity is given to all men. He alone can determine his fate. He may rise up as an eagle with the wind of knowledge, as a god he may determine his freedom and choose to reign. Perfect justice governs our hearts, weighing all things righteously. Man has no excuse, no complaints, his life is his own, blessed or cursed—will he choose life, the one who gave all? Will he recognize his heritage, his royal ancestry? If he does, he will solve the mysteries and refresh his tired bones. He will overcome and belong again. He will know he has everything and is more than he thought he'd be. His power will surge without ceasing, now and worlds to come. His creator and Father will lead him, endless life reconciled and redeemed by only He who would save, Jesus Christ. Blessed be all who hear and understand now and forevermore. To God be the Glory!

Patricia Joy

For additional copies of:

Deliverance
"The Christian's Bill of Rights"

send $9.95 + $2.25 shipping and handling to:

Vincent Xavier
1835 Center City Pky #320
Escondido, CA 92025